Family-Integrated Church

Healthy Families, Healthy Church

by J. Mark Fox

Antioch Community Church
1600 Powerline Rd.
Elon, NC 27244
(336) 586-0997
markfox@antiochchurch.cc

PRESS

This book is first dedicated to my wife, Cindy. In my wildest imaginations I cannot think of living the last 18 years of Antioch's history without you by my side. It was you, my darling, who kept me going through your prayers and encouragement, especially at times when it would have been easier to give in or give up. I also dedicate this book to my 7 children, Micah, Caleb, Hannah, Luke, Jesse, Judah & Susanna. I understand what John meant when he said "I have no greater joy than...that my children walk in truth." (3 John 4). I am doubly blessed to be a part of two very special families—my own, and our church.

I would also like to thank the people of Antioch Community Church for being eager and willing to press toward the goal for the prize of the upward call of God in Christ Jesus. You inspire me to press in and be the man of God He has created me to be. I love you all.

Thank you, finally, to my proofreaders and 'editors': Cindy Fox, Mark & Laura Leake, Dick & Sheila Orcutt, Mark & Hope Kemp, and Dennis & Polly Riddell. Your encouragement through this writing process has been immeasurable.

I have changed the names of people
involved in Antioch's past.

Table of Contents

Foreword

It was a spring Sunday morning in 2005, and we were sharing our 'thanksgivings' with each other at Antioch Community Church. A man who drives his family 90 minutes one way to worship with us every Sunday took the wireless handheld microphone and shared that one of his little boys that morning had asked as they prepared to leave the house, "Are we going to the 'food and song' church?" He was corrected immediately by his 7-year old sister who said, "No, it's called Antioch Comedy Church."

You know what? Both of those children were right. Our church is filled with songs of worship as we praise the Lord with grateful hearts every time we gather. The food is abundant as we enjoy the spiritual manna that He shares through the Word and testimony every week. We also enjoy eating together most Sundays as many families will bring a covered dish or a picnic lunch and stay after for fellowship around the tables. Comedy? Well, there's plenty of laughter at Antioch *Community* Church, not the raucous or sarcastic type, but the kind that results when family gets together. That's what we are, after all. We are part of the family of God.

This book was born out of a conference I attended in

Raleigh, NC in April of 2005. It was a regional "Uniting Church and Home Conference," and the main speakers were Scott Brown, Voddie Baucham, and Ted Seago. I met people from lots of places, including a couple from Florida who said they are desperately seeking a church that is 'family-integrated.' As my wife and I listened to them talk about what they want in a church, we were reminded (again) how blessed we are to be a part of Antioch. We realized again how God had led us over the past 18 years to be a church where biblical manhood and womanhood is celebrated and encouraged, and families are not divided up as soon as they walk in the door. We were humbled that God had allowed us to be a part of this movement back to the Scriptures, this reformation of church and family that is taking place across our nation. We did not start out to be a 'family-integrated' church. In fact, I didn't even know what that term meant until 2003, when I saw it on the Vision Forum website and realized that it described us.

I wrote this book for several reasons. First, I wrote it because I believe it may give encouragement to families who are looking to be a part of a church that honors the family. Second, I believe it may give instruction to those who are looking to be a part of a new family-integrated church plant. Third, I believe it may be helpful to pastors or people in leadership in more traditional churches but who desire to help their church move towards a family-integrated model. Finally, I am praying the book will awaken a desire in some who read it and did not even *know* they wanted to be a part of a family-integrated church!

Antioch Community Church is not perfect, not even close. As long as we have even one member, there is no hope for perfection this side of heaven! We have much to learn and a long way to go, but God is our guide and our target. This book is not about us, but about Him. May He get all the glory.

In Christ,
J. Mark Fox

CHAPTER 1

Humble Beginnings

F ive families started Antioch Community Church in March, 1987. Three were black and two were white. We were determined that *this* church was the answer to all the county's problems. We just knew that *this* church would set new records in attendance. I had dreams of a mega-church in little ol' Burlington, North Carolina, and thousands of people coming to multiple services every week. I wrote out a long term vision and it included things like a school, a huge missions outreach, a top-rate church education program, a multi-national and multi-ethnic congregation, even a Bible School or seminary. Hey, if you're going to dream, why not dream big? After all, you have to aim at the stars if you want to hit the moon, right?

We had a place to meet. It was the New Directions Evangelistic Association, in a renovated grocery store, near downtown Graham. The New Directions is a missions organization that started in 1968 when a young couple in Burlington, NC decided to take 15 or 20 young people on vacation to Mexico with them. That summer vacation led to an interracial singing group, called "The New Directions," and then an international missions organization. I had worked for the New

Directions in the summers of 1984-86, and traveled full-time as an evangelist with "Damascus Road," a ministry team that was also under the New Directions umbrella. The director of New Directions and I were friends, and I looked to him for spiritual leadership and guidance as we started this new church venture. He and his family joined us as one of the founding five.

The other three families included a man who also worked for the New Directions, a family physician, and a financial planner. We began to meet together in one of the homes every Thursday night, and I remember lots of prayer, lots of looking in the Scriptures, and lots of excitement as we dreamed about what this new work would look like.

The Antioch Church birth began in earnest on May 10, 1987-- Mother's Day. We held our first Sunday service that day beginning at the odd time of 3:00pm, because there was already a church meeting in the New Directions' building on Sunday morning and evening. We fit our schedule around theirs until they moved out in the fall of 1988.

Our Sunday School began at 2:00pm and we had classes for all ages, just as advertised! In the early days, everybody did everything and it wasn't a chore to get people to work or to serve. A new church can just about run on adrenaline for the first year or two, and ours certainly did. Not only did we offer Sunday School from the very beginning, but "Children's Church" for ages 2 and ½ to 5th grade during the sermon time as well.

On Wednesday evenings we met in homes for Bible Study and what we called 'cell groups.' We started with one but it wasn't long before a second and a third cell was needed as the little church grew.

On Thursday evenings, we gathered at the New Directions again and did what we called 'outreach.' On any given night there was a handful of people going door to door in the neighborhood behind the building, handing out tracts and witnessing if the opportunity arose. We had a food and clothes closet in the building and there was always someone organizing, collecting, or distributing the goods. We had a group in the rock room (a room literally built around a huge piece of granite) on their knees in prayer. We had a few people who were visiting shut-ins or people who had shown an interest in the church. We had people in the little patch of grass behind the building playing soccer or dodge-ball with the children of the church and the community kids who were attracted to the hubbub. We even offered a discipleship ministry, and I taught classes on what it meant to follow Christ. In short, we had LOTS going on, and our intentions were very good. We truly wanted to make a difference for the Savior.

Everything was sailing along during the first year, and new people were coming to the church nearly every week. There were five men who started the church, and four of them served as the first elders. The other helped lead worship but maintained his membership with a former church, and he did not want to make a complete break from them.

The Lord brought a fifth man in fairly soon after we began, and he became the first deacon. He enjoyed making everything hum from behind the scenes. He took care of the money, along with another brother, and he was our set-up and sound man. I knew if there was anything I needed when it came to the practical workings of a church service or an outreach, he was the man I needed to speak to. He still is.

The four of us who served the flock as spiritual shepherds recognized the gravity of our responsibility to take care of the sheep and make sure they were fed and cared for. I believe that any church, but particularly a new one, is going to be tested in the area of doctrines, and it wasn't long until it happened to us.

CHAPTER 2

A Strange Visitation

It was early in the first year that we started getting visits on Sunday afternoons from a woman who had a quiet, but mysterious, demeanor. She rarely spoke and was usually accompanied by her grown son who always appeared to be a bit uncomfortable. He reminded me of a rabbit who had been spooked a number of times. There was no husband.

I knew we were in for trouble when she first introduced herself to me after a service.

"Hello, my name is Mark Fox," I said.

"My name is Miriam White," she replied. (OK, I thought, so far so good.) Then she added, "I am the bride of Christ."

"Excuse me, ma'am, wh-what did you say?" I stammered. I knew full well what I thought she said, but I was hoping I was wrong.

"I am the bride of Christ," she repeated. I caught a glimpse of her son who was fervently studying a mole on the back of his hand. Seeing that he was not going to be any help, I leveled my gaze on the "bride."

"Mrs. White," I began, "You can be a part of the bride of Christ, but you cannot BE the bride of Christ. You see, the Bible is very clear that the church is His bride and He is coming back to get us one day to take us home to heaven. He is not coming back to get just one person, but the whole church."

She smiled at me like she was a sixth grader and I was a kid who had just graduated from kindergarten and was bragging that I could "cipher" all the way up to my sixes.

"The Lord <u>has</u> revealed to me that I am the Bride of Christ," she insisted. I was surprised she didn't reach out and pat me on the head when she said it.

Well, that conversation fizzled out pretty quickly after that, but it was one of those times when you think of all kinds of things you SHOULD have said when you get home that day. I knew we were in for trouble with Mrs. Bride, so I alerted the other elders about it at our next meeting. Sure enough, it wasn't long before it happened.

She showed up at church soon after that wearing a full length, white dress, a flowy thing that looked a lot like something a bride might wear. I whispered a warning to my wife, something like, 'Here comes the bride.'

We had just finished our time of singing praise to the Lord the very next Sunday, when I stood up to ask if anyone in the church had something to share that would encourage the body. There were a few testimonies and thanksgivings, and then the Bride in White stood up. I didn't want to be rude to her, and I didn't really have a clue what she was going to say (that's always the exciting part of having 'open sharing time' at church!), so I nodded that she could speak.

"The time of the Gentiles is over!" she exclaimed. All heads swiveled as one as every person in the congregation turned to look. "God has closed the door on the Gentiles, and they will no longer be allowed to enter the Kingdom of Heaven. Yea, I am returning to My people now," she spoke "prophetically," and "Israel will come back to the fold. But the day of the Gentiles is over."

She took a breath, I was hoping along with everyone else that she was finished, but the 'bride' was just getting warmed up.

"Not only that," she said, "The Lord says there will be a plague of ants on the earth."

There goes our church picnic at the park next week, I thought.

About this time, one of the elders (the most experienced among us) was bending over and pulling up his socks. I had no idea what that meant. *Maybe he is worried about all those ants that are going to be running wild in here any minute,* I thought.

I found out later from his wife that she knew *exactly* what the sock-pulling was all about. "Some men clear their throats when they are getting ready to stand up and say something," she said after the service. "Some men fidget in their seats or fix their hair. *MY* husband pulls up his socks!"

He kept pulling and the bride kept talking.

"The ants will cover the earth as a sign of God's judgment," Mrs. Bride continued. "The hand of the Lord is against you. He is against this church because you will not submit to Him and His Spirit. The day of the Gentiles is over!"

The would-be bride looked confident, even smug, as she sat back down in her metal folding chair. I could feel the sweat trickling down the side of my face, as every head in the place snapped back to full-frontal attention. *What're you going to do, now?,* some seemed to be saying to me with a sympathetic gaze. Others communicated a clear word with one look: *Set that woman straight!* At that moment, only one thought came to my mind, and I know it was put there by the Holy Spirit. That thought was, *This church is led by elders.*

"The Bible says to **test the spirits, whether they are of God,**" (1 John 4:1) I said. "Do any of the elders have anything to say to that prophecy?"

The elder who had been getting his socks (and his thoughts) ready shot to his feet in less than a New York second and said, "Yes, I do." The swivel was immediate as all heads and eyes were turned toward this man who was the "elder brother" in the church.

"This prophecy is clearly not from God, but is of another spirit," he said. "The Bible is clear that many things must take place that have not yet taken place before the end of times can come and the age of the Gentiles is fulfilled. *The Lord is not slack concerning His promise,'* as Peter said, *'but is longsuffering toward us, not willing that any should perish but that all should come to repentance.* (2 Peter 3:9) There is also no Scripture that would support her prophecy that God will bring a plague of ants on the earth. This is not a word from the Lord."

He sat down, I thanked him for sharing that correction, and everyone (almost) was nodding with satisfaction. Everyone, that is, except for the lady in white. She was looking through me with a steely gaze, a slight smile curling her lips, and I sensed that this little skirmish was just getting started. No sooner had I started preaching that I noticed motion.

You know how your eye tends to go to the moving object when everything else is still? My eyes were drawn like a magnet to the spurned, would-be prophetess, and I couldn't believe what I was seeing. She was rolling her hands around in the air in front of her in a way that resembled a sorceress's incantation, and then she was pointing both hands at me as if they were six shooters, thumbs up, index finger extended, other fingers cocked. Roll, roll, roll, shoot, shoot. Roll, roll, roll, shoot, shoot. This went on for about a minute and I tried, I really did, to keep preaching. But I knew I was going to have to stop and deal with this before she got even more disruptive. Already some of the teens nearby were beginning to gape, elbow their Dads, and point.

I stopped preaching and said, "Mrs. White, you're going to have to stop doing that, or you will have to leave."

Again, the swivel happened in unison as those in the front (who had no idea what was going on) turned to look.

She just continued the motion with a mocking smile that said, "Make me."

I looked at the other elders and without a word two of them got up and made their way to the rolling, shooting 'prophetess.' They leaned over and whispered to her that she would not be allowed to continue to disrupt the service, and would she like to go outside to the foyer and talk? She got up, still smiling, and walked out the front door. Her son, hat in hand and looking like this was not the first time this had happened, sat still for several minutes after I had resumed preaching. Then, he got up sadly, and walked out.

I was shaken after that incident and couldn't begin to tell you what I said after that. My bet is there is no one who was at Antioch that day who could tell you, either. But what preached the loudest was the response of the elders when a false prophet was in the fold. Rather than allowing the wolf to have its way, or trying to coexist with the wolf so as not to "lose" a church member (she was not a member, but you get my drift), the elders had exercised one of the oldest and most-often ignored practice—church discipline. That made an impression on the young congregation and built their trust in us, their spiritual leaders. It also impressed a truth on me that I already knew but *love* to be reminded of—the responsibility for leadership is not upon my shoulders alone but is spread among a group of godly elders. When there is a need for reproof or correction, we seek the Lord for wisdom and act on what He tells us. (More about church discipline in a later chapter)

Paul said to Titus that he was leaving him in Crete to *set in order the things that are lacking, and appoint elders.* (Titus 1:5) What do the elders do? Among other things, Paul said it is the responsibility of an elder to know the Word of God *that he may be able, by sound doctrine, both to exhort and convict those who contradict. For there are many insubordinate, both idle talkers and deceivers,...whose mouths must be stopped.* (Titus 1:9-11)

When the elders of any church are willing to be men of God and men of the Word, and stop the mouths of those who would contradict the teaching of Scripture, the church will be blessed. That incident in the first year of ministry was a defining moment for us as a church. There would be many others along the way, and the Lord would continue to test our resolve to fully trust Him and His Word.

In fact, it wasn't long after this 'visitation' that the Lord really *did* speak to us about something. He wanted to see if we would be willing to humble ourselves.

CHAPTER 3

As Much As It Depends On You

"I think we need to go and be reconciled to our former pastor."

My heart sank as I heard those words come from the mouth of one of the founding elders. We were having a leadership meeting at his house one Sunday night. We had eaten together and then convened in the living room for Bible Study and prayer. As we were praying, this man began to weep quietly. After a few minutes, he said the words that I had to ask him to repeat.

"I think we need to go and be reconciled to our former pastor," he said again. "I believe the Lord wants us to do this so that we can move forward in peace."

I knew he was right. There was no doubt in my mind that this was a word from the Lord to us, because we knew the relationship we had with our previous church was not right.

None of us had taken it lightly when we left. There had been much prayer. We had sought the Scriptures. We had fasted. We had even asked the elders of our former church if we could be sent out as a church plant, as a "daughter" church. They refused. Finally, we had left, believing in our hearts that we had no choice and that God was calling us to come out from them. But there was so much hurt on both sides.

One of my friends said, "It feels like a divorce." Others said of us who'd left, "Who do they think they are? They had no right to leave our church!" There was an underlying rumbling in all of us, and many times the constant talk about "What they are saying about us," or "What are they doing now; can you believe it?" seemed to dominate our conversations. It sapped our energy, made us feel guilty, stirred our righteous indignation, and left us confused and unfruitful.

We knew that it was Jesus who said,

> *Therefore if you bring your gift to the altar, and there remember that your brother has something against you, leave your gift there before the altar, and go your way. First be reconciled to your brother, and then come and offer your gift.* (Matthew 5:23-24)

We talked and prayed for a long time that night, and decided on a plan that we believed would please the Lord. Each one of us in leadership would write a letter to the pastor of our former church, asking for his forgiveness for anything we had done wrong. We did not believe that we had been wrong to leave the church. We knew that God sometimes multiplies through division. But we also recognized that we had made some mistakes in *how* we left. We knew that the heart *is*

> *deceitful above all things, and desperately wicked* (Jeremiah 17:9),

and the source of some of the hurt in both churches was our pride.

So, we purposed in our hearts to write a letter that very next week. We would be specific, we would be contrite, and we would be prayerful that God would heal the rift.

22

I remember the story in 2 Kings 6 of Elisha's junior prophets building a larger place for all of them to live. They had outgrown their prophets' chambers and Elisha told them to go ahead and build another. He went with them and as they were building, one of the prophet's iron ax head fell off as he was cutting down a tree, and it plunged into the Jordan River. He cried out to Elisha for help, and the prophet of God asked him, "Where did it fall?" When the junior prophet showed Elisha the spot, the man of God cut a stick and threw it in the river where the ax head had fallen. Then the miracle happened. The IRON ax head floated to the top of the river, and Elisha told junior to pick it up.

I will never forget hearing Stephen Olford preaching on this passage and making the point that "the place of departure is the place of recovery." To find something we have lost, we need to go back to the place we last had it. To be restored in fellowship with God is not rocket science. He has made it very simple. We must confess where we took a wrong turn if we are going to get back on the right road. He said,

If we walk in the light as He is in the light, we have fellowship with one another, and the blood of Jesus Christ His Son cleanses us from all sin. (1 John 1:7).

Our desire was to walk in the light and to be restored in fellowship with our former church. So, we sent the letters.

It wasn't long before we got our reply. The pastor received our letters and wrote us back to say that he wanted to meet with each one of us, one at a time. We were to come to his house, where he had an office in a separate building in the back yard, and he would hear us out.

There have been some scary moments in my life. I had surgery when I was 12 years old, and I still remember the terror I felt as the nurse put the mask over my face and asked me to start counting backwards from 100. I was ushered into the principal's office when I was 17 years old, having just gotten into a fist fight in history class, which I started, and which resulted in my two front teeth being knocked out. I was involved in my first car crash, also at the age of 17. It was my fault, and I will never forget that phone call home to tell my Dad what I had done. I will also never forget the knock on the door just a few months later, when my Dad was served with a law suit because of my wreck.

These were all hair-raising moments.

But would you believe me if I told you they paled in comparison to the meeting I had with my former pastor? I remember turning into his driveway and my heart felt like it would pound all the way through my chest. My palms were moist, my mouth felt like cotton, my breath was shallow. It's a wonder I didn't pass out right there on his doorstep!

He led me down the path to his back yard retreat, and we entered and closed the door.

Then the greatest thing happened. He smiled at me and told me that he forgave me. He shared some concerns he had over the way we left and about the new work that we had started, but the bottom line was that we were forgiven. He prayed with me, and I floated back to the car, feeling maybe 20 pounds lighter.

The other Antioch elders had a similar experience. When we gathered to share our experiences, we rejoiced at the good news that as we obeyed, God supplied His grace for reconciliation. We could turn our sails into the wind of His Holy Spirit now and receive His power and direction.

Did that end all of the strife between the members of the two churches? I wish I could say that it did. But one night months after we had met with the pastor, the leaders were discussing the tension that still existed between us in some areas and with some people. I had been reading in Romans and had just read this verse:

If it is possible, as much as depends on you, live peaceably with all men. (Romans 12:18).

Our desire should be to live peaceably with all men. To that end, we must do everything that depends on us to make that happen. But do you see how Paul started the verse? "If it is possible" implies that sometimes it is not! You simply cannot have peace with someone who is bound and determined to see you as an enemy until the day he dies. Reconciliation requires two willing parties. One man cannot reconcile with another unless the other wants to be reconciled with him.

As much as we wanted to live in peace, we had done all we could and had to let it go at that. We determined that as far as Antioch was concerned, we weren't on the 'outs' with anyone or any church. God had work for us to do and an enemy to fight, and the last thing we wanted was to spend all our time and energy trying to make peace with someone who was *on our side* but would not forgive.

I am blessed to be able to say that the strife we went through for many years did end. Both of the churches have been through many changes, but God has been faithful to keep both lamp stands burning and to use us to advance His kingdom. To God alone be the glory!

The next big test for Antioch came just a few years later.

CHAPTER 4

What the Devil is Going On?

I believe it was Vance Havner who said once that when the devil shows up at church, you can usually find him in the choir loft. Well, Antioch has never had a choir, much less a loft! But we have always enjoyed music and worshiping God in song, and we have been richly blessed with many talented and committed worshipers. We have also tried hard to give people opportunities to minister in song.

The problem occurred in 1992 when the elders decided we would have a sign-up sheet for special music. That's right, anybody who wants to sing a special song during the service just needs to sign up ahead of time! We put a clipboard on a table in the sanctuary, with the Sundays and Wednesdays listed and a line beside each one. 104 Sundays and Wednesdays, no waiting.

We believed at the time that only those who had a true heart and a desire to honor the Lord (and bless the people) would sign up. Once again, what we lacked in wisdom, we tried to make up for with sincerity.

At first, the plan worked pretty well. There were a few who signed up and ministered in song, and we expected them to. After all, they were the talented ones and the people who had sung before. But we encouraged others to use their gift to edify the body, and we probably went a bit overboard to try and coax the shy ones to the front. "You don't have to sing like an angel," we said, "you just have to want to make a joyful noise and worship the Lord!" We were sincere in that, and I still believe that though not all vocal chords are created equal, God looks at the heart. He is much more pleased with a croaky chorus from a clean heart than a mellifluous melody from a malodorous heart.

It wasn't too long before we noticed that a couple of people in the church were signing up and singing on a regular basis. These were not the most talented of singers, but that was OK. We had encouraged the saints to sing, and they were doing just what we asked. But something seemed amiss. There suddenly appeared to me and some of the other leaders and our wives that there was a spirit of performance in the services. It would not have been more obvious to me if the singers had worn shirts or blouses that said, "Look at me! Listen to me!"

The problem was compounded by the fact that the two singers that were causing us the most consternation also had the least amount of ability. Yes, God looks at the heart, we said in elders' meetings. But He also gave us ears, and ours were hurting a bit. What were we to do? We had created this dilemma with our own plea to the congregation to step forward and stop hiding that light under a bushel. How could we correct the situation without causing hurt feelings and throwing a wet blanket over the people's willingness to step out and serve the body when asked to do so?

We decided on a plan. We would have a "Worship Conference" at Antioch and invite all of those in the church who were involved in music in any way to attend. It was a Friday night and a Saturday morning conference, at the church building, and all who fancied themselves as singers or musicians came.

There were three elders at that time (one of the founders was too busy in itinerant ministry to be an effective elder, and one had left to go to another church), and two of us took turns teaching the material. We looked at what Jesus said to the woman at the well, that God Himself is *seeking* worshipers who will worship Him in spirit and in truth (John 4:23). We looked at 1 Corinthians 13 and exhorted the singers and musicians to examine their hearts and see if God's love was being perfected in them. We discussed spiritual gifts and physical talents and how God has gifted some for certain ministries but not all. There are some who are called to preach, though all of us are called to be a witness and present the gospel with all who will listen. In the same way, there are some who are called to sing solos in a way that exhorts and encourages the body, but all of us are called to make a joyful noise and come into His presence with singing. (Psalm 100:2) We talked about the way the gifts work in the body of Christ and that if one of us is operating outside his gifting, the body is not edified the way it would be if all were operating in their spiritual gifts.

That's about when it happened. One of the ladies who had been singing a lot and really didn't seem to have the heart for worship nor the gift for singing, asked a question.

"Would you tell us, then, who you think the people at Antioch are who have this gift of encouragement in special music?" she asked.

I looked at the other elders, kind of knitting my brow, my mind racing ahead to try to play through the possible answers here and what the result would be for each one. But once again, lack of wisdom ruled the day. We shrugged and gave her the list.

Her name was not on it. Neither was her friend's name.

Now, if I could go back in time and answer that question again, I would have handled it very differently. I would have said something like, "Rather than us coming up with a list of people who can sing, and therefore an implied list of those who cannot, we would rather you do something for us. We would like for all of you to take this information home and to your prayer closet. Each one of you go before the Lord and ask Him what your response should be. We believe that God is not only able but He is quite willing to give each of us the answers to our questions. He is simply waiting for us to ask."

Hindsight is 20/20, and in this case I have no idea what would have happened even if we *had* encouraged such soul-searching and seeking after God. But I do know what *did* happen!

These two women were so angry and wounded by our perceived 'snub' of them and their gifts, they told their husbands and then they left the church. But not before they could talk to several other families. These families took up an offense for the two women and the elders spent the next several months just going from one house fire to another. By the time the smoke cleared, we had lost 5 or 6 of the 25 families that were attending at the time.

One of the elders said, as we were discussing the fallout, "You know, when the flesh gets pinched, sometimes it squeals."

After I stopped laughing I pondered that for a long time. How many times have I reacted to something my wife or a brother in the church says to me, only because it is the truth and it exposes my heart of flesh? How many times have I tried to rally others to my defense and have been guilty of putting a stumbling block in their way, an offense, a "skandalon?"

Jesus said,

It is impossible that no offenses (skandalon) should come, but woe to him through whom they do come!
(Lu 17:1)

What did we learn from that event? First, a church is a family, and God has called us to love each other. That happens a great deal in a happy, healthy family. He has also called us to discipline each other. The son who is not disciplined by his father, according to the Word of God, is not *loved* by his father! (Hebrews 12:5-6) Love includes discipline and discipline must be done in love. In this case, I believe our mistake was that the parties in question did not know they were being disciplined. They just felt singled out and shamed. Again, if I could replay that scene, I believe we would have talked to each of the women about their heart motives and encouraged them to find another way to honor the Lord with their gifts. The worship conference was an attempt to avoid a head-on collision, but the plan backfired and perhaps caused more grief.

The second thing we learned from the event was that music will almost ALWAYS be at the center of a controversy or two in the church. Maybe it's because Lucifer was a musical angel before his rebellion and fall, maybe it's because music stirs the soul and therefore the passions, maybe it's because *sometimes* those who want to sing simply want to be seen.

Don't get me wrong. We have some wonderful musicians at Antioch. We always have. They are godly people who love to worship God with a song and play it well, as the Scripture commands: ***Sing to Him a new song; play skillfully with a shout of joy.*** (Psalm 33:3) I praise God for their hearts of passion and their attention to excellence in their craft. God loves music and created it for our pleasure and for His.

I know one of the controversies that is raging through the churches today in America is whether we should allow drums in the church. Or whether we should sing songs that have a beat. (Actually, *all* songs have a beat!) Or whether we should only sing hymns and 'slow' choruses. I will not presume to be able to solve that dilemma. But I will say this.

I don't believe the style of music, within reason, should be an issue that divides us.

If God looks at the heart (1 Samuel 16:7), then it is the heart of the worshiper that pleases God, not the style of music he is playing. I believe that there is evidence in Scripture that God allows for instrumentation, God enjoys variety, and that God is pleased with a heart that offers praise to Him, even if it is loud and upbeat. But we will not solve this issue in this book.

For that reason, I would say that if music style is a requirement for you, find a church that preaches the gospel and models Christ-like character and has the type of music you enjoy. Don't go to one that has everything you love except the music and then set your face to *change* the church and win them to your own conviction concerning music styles. Paul said, ***Who are you to judge another's servant? To his own master he stands or falls.*** (Romans 14:4)

About the time that God whittled down our numbers a bit, something very exciting began to take place. I love that about God. He knows just how to discipline us with one hand while giving us a hug with another.

CHAPTER 5

An Open Door

I began teaching at Elon College (now Elon University) in the fall of 1990. That was a provision of God all by itself, because our little church was struggling to pay the bills, much less the pastor. I tried to take on a part-time job to help ends meet. I sold encyclopedias door to door. I taught Adult Basic Education classes at the local Community College. I even tried my hand as a vinyl siding installer's assistant. I quickly discovered that God was not calling me to that, and my boss agreed with me!

One day I called over to Elon College to see if they had any classes in the Communications Department that needed a teacher. I have a Master's degree in Speech Communications, so I thought I might put that degree to work. Little did I know that Elon had just started a Communications Department the year before, and the man who was chairman of the department was a friend of mine I had known from Chapel Hill! He told me that, yes, they did need someone to teach a course in Public Speaking. I went over and interviewed with the Dean and the next thing I knew, I was teaching a course. The next semester they asked me to teach two. Then three. Fifteen years later, I am still there, teaching classes every Tuesday and Thursday at

Elon University as an Instructor. When I started in 1990, there were 5 or 6 faculty members in the department. Now there are over thirty, and the School of Communications is getting a national reputation as one of the finest in the land!

The door that God opened for me to teach at Elon also served to open another door as well.

It was the fall of 1992. We had invited the Elon Gospel Choir to come and perform a concert at Antioch one Sunday evening. After they sang, we sat down around the tables with them and enjoyed a covered dish supper. As we laughed and fellowshipped together, one of the young ladies from the choir said, "I like this church. I wish you were closer to campus."

Another student agreed. "Yeah, I feel welcome, here." Then she added, "Hey, would you all be willing to come and do a Sunday service on campus?"

"Sure we would, "I responded. "That would be fun and a great way to bring the gospel to the college campus."

Permission was granted by the Provost of the college for a special service and it was held in December of 1992. We met in Whitley Auditorium, a stately building that was erected around the turn of the century and had been used over the years for chapel services, classes, music recitals and lectures.

It was about a week later when I got a phone call from a student in the Gospel Choir who had attended the special worship service.

"We loved it and were wondering if your church would be willing to do it every week?"

"Every week?" I replied. "I thought this was just a one-time deal!"

"Professor Fox, I think this is just what the students need. A worship service *on campus* that everyone can walk to, and that honors the Lord. Would you pray about it?"

I agreed that this request was worthy of prayer. The very next Sunday we had a special meeting after the service to discuss the invitation. After I had explained it and the implications for our little fellowship (packing up and moving equipment to the campus every Sunday), there was a few minutes of discussion. Several said, "Yeah, we need to pray about this. This is a big step."

There was a moment of silence as we all pondered what lay before us. The silence was crushed suddenly as one brother said, "I don't know why we need to pray about it."

All eyes were fixed on him as he said, "We are called to go into all the world and make disciples, aren't we? Could we ask for a better opportunity than this, to bring the gospel to a college campus, to have an open door to the life of that community? What are we waiting on? Could this be anything but the hand of God and the hand of blessing on our little church?"

One of the pitfalls that awaits any congregation is the pitfall of insulation. It is a great temptation after a few years to just focus on "us four and no more." The typical church goes through stages, we are told, from Mission to Movement to Monument to Memorial. We started Antioch with a sense of mission, but just 5 years later we were beginning to get comfortable and complacent. We were beginning to care more about starting programs than about reaching and building people. We were getting lazy in outreach and sloppy in evangelism.

This invitation from a handful of students at Elon was just what we needed.

When we started meeting on the campus, there were about 60 people in our church. After a few years, the students outnumbered us. I was reading in Revelation one day, and a verse seemed to leap off the page. It became a "life verse" for our little congregation and a great source of encouragement to us, as well as a source of exhortation.

I know your works. See, I have set before you an open door, and no one can shut it; for you have a little strength, have kept My word, and have not denied My name. (Revelation 3:8)

Jesus is speaking here to the church at Philadelphia, the only one of the seven churches for whom He did not have a rebuke. He was pleased with them. They were pleasing to God, I believe, *because* they only had a little strength. A church that sees itself as having a little strength will more than likely look to God for His mighty power. They will most likely not rely on themselves and become puffed up. We knew we were little and our strength was small. But our confidence was in Him.

They were pleasing to God because they had kept His Word. We had pleaded with God for the five years of our existence to help us be faithful to His Word. We wanted to preach the whole counsel of God and live before the world in a way that would be unexplainable except that we were marching to a different drummer.

They were pleasing to God because they had not denied His name. By God's grace we had loved His name and been faithful to proclaim that Jesus Christ is Lord and there is no other name under heaven given unto men by which we must be saved! (Acts 4:12, paraphrased)

God opened a door for our little church. The Provost agreed to the eight students' request that Antioch Community Church be allowed to present a service of worship in Whitley Auditorium every Sunday morning that school was in session. It became our home (except for a few temporary moves to other places on campus) for nine years.

God opened a door that no man could shut. There were times during our nine year mission that we believed the school was going to shut us down. Like the time a young Jewish student professed faith in Jesus Christ as his savior and asked to be baptized. Or the time a young coed professed faith in Jesus Christ and asked to be baptized. In each case I heard from the father, and he was not calling to thank me for the new direction his son or daughter was now taking!

There were also some very exciting transformations that took place in students' lives. I wish I had a dollar for every time a student said to me, "Hey, I never stayed awake through a whole sermon before. Thanks!"

There were young girls who had come to college determined that they would never ever be married. Then they spent time with the families in our church, and they saw the marriages as pictures of Christ and the church. They saw husbands and wives loving each other, serving each other, and it changed their hearts. Some of the students were almost 'adopted' into families for their four years at school. They could be found doing their laundry, babysitting, studying, or just hanging out with their 'family' at any given time!

There were young girls who had come to college convinced that there were *already* too many people in the world, so they were not going to have children. Then they were invited into one of our homes for a meal after church, and it changed their lives. There were young people who stumbled into our service on Sunday morning after a night of drinking or other self-indulgences, and they were wiping the tears away and repenting by the end of the service. There were students who came to our little church on the campus who had grown up in dead churches full of pretenders, where church was always a spectator sport that one just endured to get his 'religion card' stamped for the week. They came a time or two to *Celebration!* (the name we gave our campus ministry), and their church experience was changed for the rest of their lives. They saw families sitting together, they heard testimonies from Dads about how they wanted to be the men God had called them to be for their family's sake, they heard students standing up during 'thanksgiving time' and talking about how they were living for Jesus on the campus. They walked away from it with a new vision for what church is supposed to be about. They were invited into the family for a celebration or two, and the rest, as they say, is history.

Even today, nearly four years after our last worship service on the campus, I still hear from students whose lives God touched through our little church. They are all over the world. When God called us to go into all the world, He literally said "as you go," make disciples of all nations. He called us to the campus for nine years, and as we went, He brought the world to us.

One of the greatest works God did in Antioch during this time period in our history was to confirm what we already believed. God has a missionary heart and sent His only Son to the mission field to die for the world. We are also called to go and to pray and to help others go. That was one of the reasons we named the church Antioch in the first place. The first church at Antioch in Acts 13 was a sending church. The leaders were praying one day and the Holy Spirit told them to send out two of their leaders as missionaries! That's how Paul was sent out and ultimately became the greatest missionary the world has ever known. But he always came back to report to his home church, his sending church, the church at Antioch.

We looked at the period between September and May for nine years as our missionary time. We were on 'furlough' during the summer, meeting off campus in various locations, re-charging our spiritual batteries, getting prepared to go on the campus again.

I believe that God was doing a work of preparation in our hearts in those nine years that we did not even recognize until much later. We could not be a *program-driven* church while we were meeting on the campus, and did not have a facility to "call our own." Our whole world as a church was focused on people, on building relationships with students and with each other, on discipleship. We did not have the space or the energy to devote to age-segregated programs.

So, we did not have them. Instead, we were giving our lives to serve college students. Our families learned how to serve and minister together. There is one example of that family ministry that stands out in my memory.

We called them "fellowship dinners." We would send around a clipboard during the service and ask the people (students and Antioch members) to sign up if they were interested in going to someone's home for lunch or supper on a particular Sunday (usually two or three weeks out). The Antioch members were asked to put an asterisk by their name when they signed up if they were willing to host a group. We would pass the clipboard around the next Sunday and the next, and usually there would be 60-100 people signed up to attend a fellowship dinner. There would be 6-10 hosts signed up as well. So, Cindy and I (or someone else on occasion) would take the list, compare it to the last time we had fellowship dinners (in an attempt to avoid putting someone at the same house twice in a row), and then assign 2 or 3 families and 4-5 students to come to each host home on the following Sunday. We would call the hosts, give them their "names," and they would call each person and ask them to come and assign them something to bring. Sometimes the host would decide it would be a "Mexican food" dinner or "spaghetti and fixings" or "hamburgers and hotdogs." Each person would show up for the meal that Sunday with something to share.

These fellowship dinners were wonderful. The students would often call and ask if they could bring a friend or a roommate who was not on the list. Sometimes the one they brought was not a Christian, and they saw firsthand how much the church of Jesus Christ loves and serves.

The gatherings were all different. Some groups would end up in a rousing board game. Some groups would get out the guitars and sing for hours. Some would just sit in the living room after the meal and tell stories, share testimonies, and get to know each other.

Many of the host families treated this as an opportunity for their children to learn to show hospitality and to serve with cheerfulness. It was wonderful for the young people, and they got to know the college students and learned to love them. My oldest son still tells the story of his 13th birthday when 5 of his 'college buddies' from Elon came over and celebrated the occasion with us. He still keeps in touch with some of them more than 8 years later.

The church is still in touch with many of the students we ministered to. Today there are young couples in our church and around the country who met at Elon, maybe even at our church on the campus, got married, and are serving the Lord. They are raising their children to love the Lord, and they are serving Him with all their heart.

When God opens a door, no man can shut it. And when God opens a door, and we are obedient to His invitation, there will be much fruit. Fruit that remains.

As God was doing a work *through* us on the campus, He was doing a work *in* us as well.

CHAPTER 6

A Heart for Family

How many times have we said to someone who has just pulled a prank on us, "You just wait. When you *least* expect it, that's when it's going to happen."

Looking back over the nine years we were on the college campus, I can see that God was doing something in our little church when we least expected it. It was no prank, either. He was building a fellowship, a family, a group of people who loved each other and were committed to serving Him together. As we worked in the fields side by side, the Lord was knitting our hearts together and giving us a common purpose and vision. And, much to our surprise, He was bringing in laborers. He was adding to our number!

I can remember having conversations with many people during those years that went something like this.

"How's the church going?"

"Great! God has continued to open a door for us to be on the college campus, and we are having a great time ministering there."

"Are you growing?"

"Well, yeah! I mean, we had an average of 75 students every Sunday last year."

"How many adults and children are members of Antioch?"

"Uh, I think it's about 85 or so, if everybody was there at the same time. But with the students, we have over 150 on a normal Sunday. And on Family Weekend last year, we had more than 200 people there."

"Hey, that's great. But you know, Mark, you can't build a church on the backs of college students. They are fickle, they don't tithe, and some of them eventually graduate!"

"Yeah, I know. But God has called us here for a reason, and for a season, so we have to be faithful. God will take care of the rest."

That conversation, or one like it, happened multiple times. Sometimes I would counter the whole "numbers argument" with one of spiritual growth. And I do believe that the growth of a church is much more a measurement of spiritual maturity than it is of nickels and noses. God has always worked through remnants while the multitudes have abandoned Him and gone their own merry way. If God were impressed with numbers, He would have chosen Egypt, not Israel.

But at the same time I was trumpeting our spiritual growth, I was crying out to God for help.

"Lord, you said in Matthew 9:38 that we should pray the Lord of the harvest to send out laborers, and that's what I am here to ask you for today. Lord, the fields are white, the fruit is dying on the vine, the harvest is plentiful but the workers are few. Lord, please send us some workers! The problem is not the work, there's plenty of that to go around. The problem is there are not enough workers. But You are faithful, Lord. You will give us strength to do what a church twice our size could do. Because our strength is small, Your strength has to be great, Lord! You are our Rock, You are our Fortress, You are a Strong Tower that we can run to and you will protect us from the evil one and provide for us in a desert place. You are great and glorious, Lord, and worthy to be praised. Not unto us, O Lord, not unto us, but to *Your* name give glory! "

Sometimes by the time this prayer session was over I was singing or shouting praises to the Lord, and He had encouraged me that we were right where we needed to be, and we were doing just what we needed to be doing. Is there any place sweeter than the middle of the will of God? Even when that center spot is in the crosshairs of the enemy, and it usually is, or when that center spot lands us in a fiery furnace or a den of lions or in the Valley of Elah facing a giant, it's still a *good* place to be. It may mean persecution, it may even mean death, but as Paul said, "to live is Christ, but to die is gain (*more* Christ)!"

Lest I lead you to the wrong impression, for every time I prayed and trusted God and rejoiced over His provision for Antioch, there were probably two times or more that I fretted and worried and compared our church to the one on the other side of town that was having to add on to their sanctuary once a year to accommodate growth. Much of the time I did *not* do it right, but God was faithful to bless Antioch in spite of me.

As I looked around one day I realized that God was bringing in families and singles who had a heart to reach the lost. He was also bringing in fathers who wanted to raise up Godly children and mothers who wanted to be their husband's helpmate. He was raising our children around us with a heart for ministry, with a desire to know God and His Word, with a passion for defending their faith in an increasingly wicked and perverse generation.

I attribute a large part of that to the fact that two of the elders of the church at that time, including myself, were homeschool dads. The other leaders of the church, whether they were deacons or served in the music ministry, were also faithful to the biblical mandate that fathers have to train and disciple their own children, and that training was beginning to produce good fruit in our children. Others were beginning to see the fruit. Suddenly the word was getting around that Antioch was a church with a mission to reach the college campus and with the commitment to godly families.

Let me hasten to say, however, that though most of the families at Antioch are homeschoolers, it is not required! One of our most faithful couples raised three beautiful daughters, and all of them went to the public schools. All three are serving the Lord today, and their father has always been one of our leaders. I cannot imagine what Antioch would have been without this man who has been as much of a Barnabus (*son of encouragement*) to me as anyone I have ever known.

I believe that a church should be built on the gospel of Jesus Christ. He is our foundation. Our fellowship is not built on whether we homeschool our children, or whether we have a TV in the house, or whether we allow a daughter to go to college, or whether our worship on Sunday includes drums or bass guitar.

But because God has made us a family, not a corporation, there is much that we will need to agree on, if we are to have peace. Amos 3:3 says, *Can two walk together unless they are agreed?* When it comes to the essentials of the faith, we must be agreed. I believe also that for the church to walk together in unity, we must also agree on the direction, or the vision, of the church.

It was becoming clearer to us as we grew up in the Lord that God was changing the vision of the church. We had started with the idea that we could be all things to all people, and the key was to have the right people in the right programs, and then we would have the right results. But God began to change our hearts. We began to see that the heart of the church was family, that God had called us to relate to one another as brothers and sisters, and to the elders as fathers. We began to understand that the light that shines the farthest shines the brightest at home. We began to catch on to the revelation that God's purpose for "youth ministry" is to turn the hearts of the fathers to their children and the hearts of children to their fathers, to paraphrase the last verse in the Old Testament.

God was giving us a vision for raising up Godly families and being committed to making a difference not just in the world we live in now but in the world our grandchildren will live in, should the Lord tarry. God was birthing in us a desire for what Doug Phillips would refer to later as "multi-generational ministry."

At the same time God was bringing in like-minded families, He was stirring the pot in some of our programs. It would be a time of pruning.

CHAPTER 7

4th Grade Boys, Anyone?

⸙

As I said earlier, Antioch began like a house afire, and what we lacked in maturity we tried to make up for in zeal and energy. But, as we have found out through the years, there is no substitute for maturity and wisdom. Don't take my word for it; ask the young men in our church.

You see, every year in the fall we have a Men's Retreat, traditionally at the beach. We rent a large beach house on the ocean and pile in there with as many as 40 or more fathers and sons. The sons have to be 12 years old to come with their Dads (more about the significance of that age in a later chapter), and boys begin to count the days until their twelfth birthday, beginning around the age of ten!

We arrive on Thursday afternoon or evening, and stay until Saturday. The focus of the weekend is spiritual renewal and includes times of Bible Study, praise and worship, prayer, sharing and accountability. But there is also a healthy dose of free time for fishing, golf, shell-collecting, and a favorite annual tradition…the football game! Yes, every year the young men (ages 21 and younger) take on the older men (everybody else) in a game of beach football. Every year the result is the same. The older men win.

It's not because we have more speed. We don't. It's not because we have more zeal. We don't. It's not because we have more energy. We definitely do not.

It's because we have more wisdom. We know how to win. The greybeards got that way through years of experience. And wisdom trumps speed, zeal, and energy any day of the week! Even when zeal holds weekly practices every Sunday for a year after church. Even when zeal devises plays and plans and strategies. Even when zeal really, really wants to finally beat the older men. (My wife says maybe we always win because the fathers play rough, and the young men don't, out of honor and fear! Hey, maybe the young men are wiser than I thought…☺)

There *is* one good thing you can say about zeal. It doesn't give up. It keeps coming back for more, and wisdom is always ready to oblige.

As we matured as a fellowship, we began to realize something that would change the philosophy of ministry at Antioch Community Church. We began to see that though our programs for children had been started with good intentions, and God had used them in spite of the fact that it was not His perfect will, the time had come to change.

We came to the conclusion a good while ago at Antioch that a presupposition we had brought into the church when we planted it was not biblical.

We had believed, most of us, that children will learn best at church if they are separated from their parents when they come in the front door and are sent to classrooms where there will be trained and qualified teachers eagerly waiting to pour their lives into these young ones! Most of us came by that knowledge honestly. We had grown up going to age-segregated classrooms in the public schools. We had also grown up going to age-segregated classrooms in the church, a la Sunday School, Pioneer Clubs, Royal Ambassadors, and more. We had assumed that it was right and biblical to separate children according to age groups, sequester them in different parts of the building, and teach them in a classroom of their peers.

You know what God used to move us away from that model? We ran out of "trained and qualified teachers eagerly waiting to pour their lives into young ones," ESPECIALLY young pre-pubescent boys. We had started with lots of zeal and energy where everybody was willing to do anything. But as we aged, and fatigue began to set in more quickly, we got a little pickier about what we were willing to do. Suddenly a classroom full of 4th grade boys did not have the missionary appeal that it once did. The announcement on Sunday morning or Sunday night or Wednesday night began to sound like a broken record: "Folks, if we are going to be able to continue to have Pioneer Clubs, someone will have to step up and fill the following slots." It got to the point that one day, one of the elders said in our weekly leadership meeting, "Maybe we are not *supposed* to continue Pioneer Clubs."

We had grown weary of trying to fill an ever-present void in this Sunday School classroom or that Pioneer Club age-level. More than that, however, we began to realize that we were violating what James said in Chapter 3, verse 1:

My brethren, let not many of you become teachers, knowing that we shall receive a stricter judgment.

The problem we were running into was that in our desperation to fill a "need," we were asking people to teach who did not have a God-given call or ability, and that caused frustration for them, for their students, for their students' parents, and for the elders!

So, we got out of the business of age-segregated classrooms, not for the reasons we don't have them now, but for the ones that God used at the time. He always will use what is available to get our attention, won't He? You remember that

49

God used a burning bush on the backside of the desert to get Moses' attention. When the would-be deliverer turned aside to look at a bush that was burning but not being consumed, God spoke.

In our case, God didn't use a burning bush but a bunch of burned-out teachers to flag us down and cause us to re-think the whole age-segregated learning model. We changed the direction of our ministry to children almost immediately, and we have never looked back.

I can hear what some of you are thinking, because I have heard many say it out loud: "Does that mean you don't ever have *any* programs?!

Let's look at that subject in the next chapter.

CHAPTER 8

Let's Build People, Not Programs

I remember hearing years ago about how a wall-eyed pike could be conditioned into unbelief. You see, the pike's favorite food is a minnow. You drop a minnow in a tank with a pike, and it is time for a minnow funeral. An experiment was conducted where a glass partition was put in the tank, dividing it in half, with the pike on one side and the minnow on the other. At first, the pike took off after that minnow like a preacher after a piece of fried chicken. The pike slammed into the glass! Undaunted, the pike got up a full head of steam, licking his chops in anticipation of a fish fry, and wham! He hit the glass again. And then again. And again. Finally, he gave up. His little fish brain had been reprogrammed to believe a lie: "I can't eat minnows anymore. It hurts like crazy whenever I try. Just can't do it."

Then the proof that the conditioning was complete; the glass partition was removed. The minnow swam cautiously, slowly towards the pike, knowing his little life was a nano-second away from being a distant memory. He swam closer to his predator. No response. The pike didn't even give the minnow a look. Why should he? He believed he couldn't have it, so why torment himself by eyeballing the tasty morsel?

The truth had not changed; the pike *could* eat the minnow. However, he now suffered from unbelief, and went hungry because of it. He had believed a lie.

I know we humans are much higher up the food chain. Hey, we EAT the pike that eats the minnow (or wishes he had)! The truth is, however, that we can be conditioned into believing a lie just as easily, and I believe the church today has believed LOTS of them.

I believe one of those lies says, "A healthy church is a program-driven church." We can see the evidence of this lie all around as churches compete with one another to have the most programs to offer the community. The winning church is the one that has something every night for the people to do, keeps them hustling off to this meeting or to that event, and brags that they are "running 400 in Sunday School."

I like to have fun with pastors; we tend to be a very insecure bunch. I was at a pastors' conference once and a fellow pastor I had just met asked me, "So, how many are you running in Sunday School?" I didn't crack a smile; in fact, I frowned and said, "Oh, we really discourage running at church, during Sunday School or anytime. Someone could get hurt." There was a slight pause as I saw this pastor trying to figure out which planet I had beamed in from. Then he chuckled nervously and said, "Ha! That was a good one."

After another pause, he said it again, "So, how many ARE you running in Sunday School?" I smiled this time and said, "We don't have Sunday School." Now he was convinced that there was something wrong with me and pursued his line of questioning until he got the answer he wanted: how many people we have (which happened to be fewer than his number). Satisfied that his church was superior, he felt free to challenge me on Sunday School. I simply told him that at Antioch, we believe our primary responsibility is to train fathers to love and lead their families, and Sunday School can sometimes interfere with that. I didn't even broach the subject of age-segregation and the problems it causes.

In the 18 plus years we have been a church, I cannot remember a single time when anyone has called and asked me, "Does the church there exist for the glory of God?" Or, "Do the people there REALLY love each other and practice biblical fellowship?" Or, "Do you believe and preach and practice the Word of God there at Antioch?" Or, "Is your church led by a mature and spiritually healthy plurality of elders?"

The questions I get instead are, "What do you do for the children?" Or, "What do you do for the youth?" Or, "What do you do for the babies?"

Now, these parents are not bad people, in fact they have a legitimate concern for the spiritual training of their children. For that, we praise God, though we may differ with some parents about how a church is to best nurture children and youth. We LOVE children and young adults here at Antioch, and more importantly, we believe God loves them and has a plan that includes them in advancing His Kingdom. The primary way He will do that, we believe, is through the family, specifically through the leadership of the father.

So, when I get these phone calls, I am liable to say, "We have about 40 fathers here who love God and are learning how to love their wives and their children. Would you like to come and be a part of a church that believes it is the father's responsibility to lead and teach and disciple his own family?" Do you know what we are finding? There are more and more out there who DO want that, but it can be a difficult transition for some fathers *and* mothers. They have been conditioned by the program-driven church to believe that it is NOT the responsibility of the father to do spiritual training. If anybody does it, it should be the Sunday School teacher, they have been taught. And if anything happens at home, well, that's Mom's responsibility!

On the contrary, Deuteronomy 6:4-9 is a command to the fathers in Israel to love the Lord with all their heart, and the measure of that love will be the training of their children to do the same. God says to Dads,

You shall teach them (His commands) diligently to your children, and shall talk of them when you sit in your house, when you walk by the way, when you lie down, and when you rise up. (Deuteronomy 6:7)

Proverbs was written by a young father who saw it was his responsibility under God to train his son.

My son, hear the instruction of your father, and do not forsake the law of your mother. (Proverbs 1:8)

Solomon calls on his son again in chapter 2 to listen to his teaching:

My son, if you receive my words, and treasure my commands within you... (Proverbs 2:1).

Again in chapters, 3,4,5,6 and 7, Solomon begins his teaching with a word to his son! Solomon did not hand over his responsibility for spiritual training to the priests and the scribes; he did it himself. In the New Testament, the principle is repeated:

And you, fathers, do not provoke your children to wrath, but bring them up in the training and admonition of the Lord. (Ephesians 6:4)

A program can accomplish a specific task; there is no doubt about it. The problem is that many programs accomplish that task and are no longer needed, but because the people have been conditioned to believe that the program is vital to their spiritual growth and well-being, then it must be continued at all costs! What began perhaps as a movement of God quickly becomes a monument and finally a memorial. There is no life there but like a perpetual care cemetery, that program must be trimmed and maintained forever.

Most of us know that Sunday School began in England in the 1700's and the idea spread to the United States and caught on in the 1800's here. But why was Sunday School begun in the first place? It was an effort to reach out to the poor children who were not well educated, who were running wild in the streets on the "Sabbath" and profaning the day of the Lord. It was an effort at evangelism and education, and I believe God used the effort to win souls and encourage saints to reach out. But as with many programs that started out with good intentions, the purpose morphed into a place to corral young people and children so they could be kept out of trouble and possibly where they could be taught the Bible stories that every child should know.

Am I suggesting that any church that offers a Sunday School program is outside the will of God and therefore disobedient? No, I will not make that judgment. I would say, however, that most churches who offer age-segregated programs do so because they believe that is 'normal Christianity,' not because they believe it is the best way to reach children. They keep the programs in place because of the same old refrain that we have heard since time immemorial: "We have *always* done it that way." They keep Sunday School and other programs in place because they honestly believe that a church without a Sunday School program is not even a biblical church. But I would challenge them to find anything that vaguely resembles age-segregation in the Scripture. The burden of proof is on those who maintain age-segregation in the church, not on those who do not.

That kind of talk usually brings up the next question. 'Do you mean to tell me that your church never has *any* programs?!'

The answer is 'no.' We offer programs, but they are for a season and targeted to a specific purpose that has a beginning, a middle and an end. For example, we like to have a summer reading program at Antioch, and encourage the young people (ages 5-18) to read Christian classics, read their Bible daily, and memorize sections of Scripture. At the end of the summer, we have a recognition service on a Sunday morning and give rewards to those who have faithfully hidden God's Word in their hearts. Last summer the teens memorized Romans 8. This summer, they are working on 2 Timothy 2, and many have decided they will memorize the entire letter.

Now, this "program" has been successful on many levels. A young man testified in a service on Sunday morning that it was the "Summer Reading Program" that got him interested a few years back in reading his Bible on a daily basis. Does that mean, then, that we must do the reading program every year? Or, shouldn't we do it *year round*, since it is such a successful "program?" No, we would prefer to leave it up to the Lord one year at a time. We know the moment it becomes an "institution" of the church, some of its lifeblood will be drained away, and it will become a "tradition" of man rather than a movement of the Holy Spirit.

We have substituted people for programs, relationships for rituals. Instead of a Sunday School program, we have people on occasion who will come to the elders with an idea. "I want to offer a course in apologetics on Sunday morning before the worship service," three men recently proposed to the elders. The class is open to all ages, of course, and will be offered for a season. It is not a program but is an opportunity for these three men to sharpen their own thinking about how to defend the faith, and the rest of us get to learn along with them and get to know each other on a deeper level. The same is happening with the women, as they had a season in 2004 when they would meet once a month for a two-hour fellowship time and teaching. It was started by my wife because she has a burden for young moms and wants to encourage them as a Titus 2 woman. The primary goal of this monthly meeting was that these ladies develop relationships with each other that would draw them to the Lord and to the truth that is available for them in His Word. Currently, there are 10-12 women meeting weekly to go through Beth Moore's study, "Breaking Free."

The women and their daughters (12 and up) go on a yearly 2-day retreat where relationships are nurtured and the older women invest in the younger through some practical teaching. The men go on an annual retreat also, as I told you in the last chapter. We always come back home with a renewed sense of purpose and vision as men and fathers who are called into battle side by side.

There are lots of musically gifted people in our church, and as the Bible says, "the Son can only do what He sees the Father doing" (paraphrase of John 5:19). So, there are lots of sons and daughters at Antioch who love to play and sing for God's glory. Last year, three of the adults in the church who are a part of our worship team approached the elders with a request. "Could we meet with the young people who are interested and teach them about using music to worship the Lord?" We gave our blessing to the idea, and the young people began to meet with these three adults, and other parents, every Sunday after the morning service. They would eat together in a classroom while one of the adults taught from the Scriptures about what biblical worship is and how much God is interested in the heart of the worshiper. Then they would spend an hour together in the sanctuary, working on songs, drama, and even litur-gical dance together. The program is on sabbatical for the summer, but will resume in the fall with a slightly different purpose. We will be working together (with more parents involved) to prepare and produce a Christmas program that will honor the Lord.

Can there be programs in the church? Yes, but God works through people, not programs. Here's what E.M. Bounds said about it:

"We are constantly on a stretch, if not on a strain, to devise new methods, new plans, new organizations to advance the Church and secure enlargement and efficiency for the gospel. This trend of the day has a tendency to lose sight of the man or sink the man in the plan or organization. God's plan is to make much of the man, far more of him than of anything else. Men are God's method. The Church is looking for better methods; God is looking for better men... When God declares that "the eyes of the Lord run to and fro throughout the whole earth, to show himself strong in the behalf of them whose heart is perfect toward him," he declares the necessity of men and his dependence on them as a channel through which to exert his power upon the world.

What the Church needs today is not more machinery or better, not new organizations or more and novel methods, but men whom the Holy Ghost can use -- men of prayer, men mighty in prayer. The Holy Ghost does not flow through methods, but through men. He does not come on machinery, but on men. He does not anoint plans, but men -- men of prayer." (E. M. Bounds, Power through Prayer)

I would submit that there can be programs, but they must be initiated by the Holy Spirit and produced through prayer. Those who administrate them must work under the umbrella of God-given authority, and should be ready and expecting to bury the program when its purpose has been served. Otherwise, that program becomes an end in itself. When that happens, the whole church is turned upside down to the point that when a new family visits, the members salivate as they see "fresh meat" who will be able to serve in their programs.

Programs can be wonderful servants but terrible taskmasters.

There is another question that we get in today's consumer-driven culture. "What do you have for my children during the worship service?" Let's examine that in the next chapter.

CHAPTER 9

No Child Left Behind?

O n a typical Sunday morning at Antioch Community Church, I will have at least one child approach me after the service and hand me a picture he or she drew during the sermon. Sometimes it is a picture of the text I was preaching from, and sometimes it is a picture of a story I told. But it always illustrates for me one very important truth: the children are listening! Not only that, they are learning.

One spring day in 2004, I was telling a story about an incident that had occurred that week in my university classroom. The subject of Mel Gibson's film, "The Passion of Christ," came up as the students chatted with each other before class began. Several students raved about the film, saying "It was awesome," or "I couldn't watch some of the scenes." Then one of the young men in the class said, "You know, they really didn't know who they were crucifying."

"What?" a young woman asked, incredulously.

"Oh, yeah," the young man continued. "They didn't know for 400 years whether it was the so-called 'Jesus of Nazareth' or not. In fact, nobody is really sure to this day who was crucified."

Now, you have to understand. This is a Public Speaking class and we spend a good portion of the semester on persuasion. We learn a bit about Aristotelian logic, and this fellow had just violated some of the basic tenets. I couldn't let it pass.

"Where did you hear that?" I asked him.

"Professor Jones," he replied. (Not his real name) "And *he* knows what he's talking about!"

I took a deep breath, said a quick prayer, and launched into a 2-minute apologetic to establish that Jesus Christ is the Son of God. When I finished, the student said, "I shouldn't have believed Professor Jones," he said. "I should have believed *you!*"

"No!" I pleaded, "Don't believe Professor Jones *or* me, believe the source."

Now flash back to the Sunday service where I am relating this story to the congregation. As soon as I said that last line, a little boy 5 years old on the back row leaned over to his mother and said, "Mommy, what's the source?" She smiled and told him it was the Bible, the Word of God.

A few weeks after that, a little boy named Timmy told me after the service that he had accepted Jesus as His Savior. He has been coming with his family for the past 4 weeks, and this little 3 year old boy hadn't missed a word of the sermon.

We have a time for folks in the church to share testimonies or thanksgivings every Sunday, sort of an "open microphone" time. I have heard pastors say over the years that they are amazed we do that.

"You are taking a real chance," they exclaim. "What if somebody just goes into a rant, or someone shares something that is not edifying, or someone says something unbiblical!"

Guess what? All of the above has happened. But I could count those incidents on both hands. I could not *begin* to count the number of times people in the congregation have shared testimonies that have brought us to tears of joy, or repentance. I could not begin to tell you the times we have burst into praise as someone has shared a triumphant report of God's intervention in his or her life.

Do we take a risk when we open the floor to whoever would share? Oh, yes. But the greater risk is taken when we allow no one to share. That, in my opinion, turns Sunday morning into a spectator sport, where only the "qualified" are allowed to stand and minister to the family of God. Never mind that Paul said,

Whenever you come together, each of you has a psalm, has a teaching, has a tongue, has a revelation... (1 Corinthians 14:26).

Each of you, Paul said. It is the responsibility of the elders to bring order and to correct anything that is not true or biblical. But it is the responsibility of *each* member of the congregation to come to the gathering of the saints prayed up and ready to minister if the Holy Spirit gives opportunity.

For that reason, it is not unusual at all to see a child of 6 or a teenager of 16 stand up on Sunday morning at Antioch and give a testimony of praise to the Lord.

Would that happen if the children were sequestered in another room, being entertained or just 'controlled' until the adults could finish worshiping God?

I believe there is strong evidence from Scripture that when the people of God gather to worship Him, that includes the children as well. I believe that 'family-integrated worship,' where the entire family is together as we sing and hear the Word and give of our offerings and hear testimonies and love the brethren, is biblical and right.

Do you remember one of the offers Pharaoh made to Moses when Moses kept pestering him to "Let my people GO!" There had been 8 plagues, the last one being locusts. The servants of Pharaoh were sick and tired of having their lives interrupted by painful boils and lice and hail and flies and frogs and disease of their livestock, so they said to their boss:

*How long shall this man (Moses) be a snare to us?
Let the man go, that they may serve the Lord their
God. Do you not yet know that Egypt is destroyed?
(Exodus 8:7)*

You gotta' love that.

So, Pharaoh calls in Moses and Aaron once more and says,
Go, serve the Lord your God. "Wait! Hold it a minute!"
Squinty-eyed, he says, *Who are the ones who are going?*

Moses answered, *We will go with our young and our
old; with our sons and daughters, with our flocks and herds
we will go, for we must hold a feast to the Lord.* Moses says,
"We are *all* going! This was the first "no child left-behind"
program, and Moses was not about to divide up the family to
go worship the Lord.

Notice how Pharaoh, who represents the voice of the
world, responds:

*The Lord had better be with you when I let you AND
your little ones go! Beware, for evil is ahead of you. Not so!
Go now, you who are men, and serve the Lord, for that is
what you desired.*

In other words, Pharaoh was saying, "You're going to
need the Lord if I let you *and* your children go. You men can
go, but the children are MINE!"

Do you see what Pharaoh was asking Moses to do? Go
ahead, you men, leave your children here with me. I will take
care of your children, don't you worry! And we are not told
Moses' response but whatever it was, whether it was a word
or just a look, Pharaoh was told in no uncertain terms that the
children of Israel were a nation of families, and they would
die as slaves before they would allow the world to separate
them! And Pharaoh drove them out of his presence.

One of the strongest passages that I believe would
support a family-integrated worship setting is found in
Nehemiah 8. Remember what had happened in Israel? The

city of Jerusalem had been destroyed by the Babylonians and the people left behind were living among the rubble—until Nehemiah found out about it and came back with the King's blessing to rebuild the wall.

As an aside, Nehemiah was inspired by God to position the men to work on the part of the wall that was directly in front of where their own family lived. Why was that a stroke of genius? Because he knew the men would be motivated to work diligently and make sure the wall in front of their own houses was strong and secure.

The wall is rebuilt in 52 days, an absolute miracle, especially given the fact that the work was opposed by friend and foe from day one. But what happened after the wall was rebuilt and the people no longer lived in shame among the rubble? God restored worship to the city of God. Ezra came to Jerusalem and *all* the people gathered as one man in the open square so that Ezra could read the Law of God to the people of God. Who gathered?

Nehemiah 8:2, So Ezra the priest brought the Law before the assembly of men and women and all who could hear with understanding...

Then in verse 3, it says it again, and repeats with emphasis that the Word of God was read before the men and women and those who could understand, clearly making a distinction that there were three groups of people gathered together to hear the Word: MEN, WOMEN, and ALL who could hear with understanding.

What does the Bible mean "all who could hear with understanding?" Well, we're not told exactly, but many believe it meant those who could understand that someone was up there reading to them! They were able to focus their attention and their minds on what was being said. God gives us a clue in Psalm 32:9:

Do not be like the horse or the mule, which have no understanding.

So, understanding is limited to humans, but what age? Well, I don't think we can put an age on it. How many of us know that understanding is not a product of age but of maturity? I know some old people who don't have much understanding. I know some toddlers who understand a whole lot. David said in Psalm 119:104,

Through your precepts I get understanding.

Maybe our children don't have understanding precisely *because* they have not sat in the congregation with the men and women and heard the Word taught.

A few years ago I was preaching through the book of Philippians and I was discussing where Paul said we are to do all things without complaining and disputing so that we may become blameless and harmless. I was talking about how we use the tongue the wrong way so often. A man in the congregation told the story after the sermon of how that week, his son (who was 8 years old) had asked him, "Dad, if you had to do without one of these three, your eyes, your ears, or your mouth, which one would you choose to do without?" The man said he asked if he would still be able to eat if he didn't have a mouth, and his son said, yes, you could eat but you could not speak. The father thought about it and said, "I guess I would do without my ears."

The son said, "No, you should do without your mouth, because the tongue is set on fire by hell itself, and you can sin with your tongue!"

Now *that's* a child who has some understanding, wouldn't you say? There is the "snow on the mountaintop" principle at work here. Our children, even the 3 year olds, are hearing truth in the service, and it accumulates in their spirit like snow does on the mountaintop in winter. Then when the spring comes, it melts and brings nourishment to the valleys.

In his book, <u>The Future of Home Schooling</u>, Michael Farris tells the story of a church that did away with "Junior Church" during the regular worship service. During the first month that the children were integrated with their families into the regular worship service, 28 children came forward to accept Jesus Christ as Savior. Farris writes, "It is amazing that while Junior Church was an attempt to make church relevant to young children, the adult church was actually far more effective in reaching these children for salvation." (p. 89)

There are many more examples from Scripture that would support family-integrated worship, even from Jesus Himself. Matthew 19:13-14 says,

Then little children were brought to Him that He might put His hands on them and pray, but the disciples rebuked them. But Jesus said,
Let the little children come to Me, and do not forbid them, for of such is the kingdom of heaven.

Jesus ministered to the whole family, and when some parents tried to bring their children closer to receive ministry from the Lord, the disciples rebuked them, and provoked one of Jesus' strongest commands: Let them come! He didn't appoint "children's workers" and send them away, He ministered to them there, in the presence of all the congregation.

For Antioch, then, being a family-integrated church means that when we gather for worship (which includes praising God through song, hearing the Word preached, giving testimony to what He has done in our lives that week, presenting tithes and offerings to the Lord, taking communion, and prayer), we gather as one, with everyone present.

I am aware that some churches believe that even a nursery is not biblical, and I can understand that approach. At

Antioch, we encourage parents to teach their little ones to be able to sit quietly and listen to the sermon. But for those who are new to that idea, and for the sake of visitors, we provide a nursery that is staffed by qualified moms and young ladies. It is available every Sunday, only during the sermon, for those two and under. There is a speaker in the nursery so that the workers (and the babies) can hear the preaching.

May I say a word about children being disruptive in the service? I believe it is Dad's responsibility to oversee the training of his little ones. He will teach his children at home when they are very young, even 2 and 3 years old, that they are to be quiet when he is teaching the Bible to the family. He will teach them that they are also to be quiet at church when someone else is speaking to the congregation. Then when the family gathers with the others on Sundays, the wise father will reinforce what he has taught at home. If his four year old, for example, is wanting to talk loudly or do something that disrupts the service, Dad is encouraged to take him out of the service and find a quiet place where the child can be spanked or disciplined in some way. After the tears have been shed for a few minutes, Dad then brings Junior back into the service. If the child is allowed to stay out of the service during the sermon time to play on the floor in the fellowship hall or to run around outside, guess what? He has won! He got exactly what he was after. If Dad brings him right back into the service every time he acts up and gets a spanking, he will learn quickly that misbehavior does not pay, and he will give it up. As soon as he does that, DAD has won and the child will begin to hear the sermon. Of course, if the disruptive child is an infant, then you would not spank. But many parents end up standing in the foyer with a baby, soothing him and still listening to the sermon. I have also seen a young lady of 15 or so offer to go and hold the baby for a tired Mom or Dad, thus serving the body of Christ and helping to build the faith of those who witness the action.

OK, we have talked about Sunday School and programs. We have discussed a biblical rationale for children being part of the worship service every week. Now, let's jump right into the fire and answer the question of the day. What about YOUTH GROUPS?!

CHAPTER 10

"Daniels and Esthers"

O ne of the questions I get from telephone inquiries about Antioch is, "What do you have for the youth?"

I have answered it various ways. I am particularly fond of Doug Phillip's response: "We have 40 fathers."

I heard Bill Gothard say in a Pastors' Seminar years ago that the key to an effective "youth ministry" is Malachi 4:6.

And he will turn the hearts of the fathers to the children, and the hearts of the children to their fathers, lest I come and strike the earth with a curse.

Youth ministry that in any way turns children away from their fathers is not ministry at all.

There is a family visiting Antioch as I write this chapter that has 12 children. They told me that when they went and visited one church, the youth pastor walked up immediately after the service and began to introduce himself to their teens. Then he put his arm around one of the young men in the family and said to his father and mother, "He's *mine*, now!"

Needless to say, that was the last time they visited that church. But that story typifies the modern philosophy of youth ministry. Ask most "youth ministers" today what his vision of ministry is, and he will say something like, "I love teens and I want to help them to love God and each other." That doesn't sound too bad, but how are you going to do that, Mr. Youth Director?

"I am going to spend as much time as I can with them each week (apart from their parents and the rest of the church), so that we can become a family."

What? They already have a family! In fact, they have *two*. The church is a family, as well. The goal of anyone who works with young people ought to be to turn their hearts toward the Lord and toward their fathers and mothers. If we do anything to undermine the family, in the name of "building a youth group," God will not bless it, and the church will suffer as a result.

Gene Edward Veith wrote an article for <u>World</u> magazine in August of 2002 entitled "Stupid Church Tricks." In the article, Mr. Veith described some of the games that have become fads in church youth groups across the country. (Let the reader beware as I describe some of these in detail).

"A youth leader chewed up a mixture of dog food, sardines, potted meat, sauerkraut, cottage cheese, and salsa, topped off with holiday eggnog….he then spit out the mixture into a glass and encouraged the members of the youth group to drink it!"

That little game led to a lawsuit in Indiana.

When asked about it, the youth director said that this "gross-out" game "was just for fun, and that the church forced no one to participate."

If you go to the website for *The Source for Youth Ministry*, you will see a category for games. One sub-category is called "Sick and Twisted Games." There are also numerous games that encourage teenage guys and girls to interact in ways that appeal to the sensual.

"Leg Line Up: have girls feel boys' legs to identify who is who. Some of (the games) have odd homosexual subtexts, like 'Pull Apart,' in which guys cling to each other, while the girls try to pull them apart."

There is a game where the youth director asks the young people to line up. Each person brushes his teeth with the same toothbrush and spits into the same cup. The last person in line drinks what is in the cup.

I am sorry to be so graphic, but I believe that we need to acknowledge that some, not all, youth groups would employ such heinous tactics in an effort to win kids over and create a community. But at what price? This is how Veith summarizes the effect such mindless games have on the young participants:

"What do the teenagers learn from these youth group activities? Nothing of the Bible. Nothing of theology. Nothing of the cost of discipleship. But they do learn some lessons that they can carry with them the rest of their lives: Lose your inhibitions...Give in to peer pressure...Christianity is stupid."

I am not attempting to paint all youth groups and all youth ministers with a broad brush. I believe God has raised up some men and women who genuinely have a heart to love young people into the Kingdom of God and to disciple them in the truth. But there are many who do not have that as their agenda, so we must beware!

We decided years ago at Antioch that God works through the family and our attention should be to encourage fathers to train up godly children, and to encourage mothers to nurture their young "olive plants" and teach them about God. We decided that we would try and equip fathers to teach, and give them a vision for leading their families in pursuing the knowledge of God. We decided that we would avoid activities that would simply throw teenagers together just to 'hang out,' but whenever we did anything aimed at the teens, we would involve the fathers and the mothers.

A lot of what we believe about young men and women has been informed by what we believe to be biblical truth:

according to the Scriptures, there are three stages of development in our lives. We are born as infants and grow as children until we are 12 or 13 years old. At that time, according to the Scriptures, a Jewish boy or girl would become an adult.

Jesus was 12 when he was brought to Jerusalem by His parents where He participated with them in the Feast of the Passover as an adult. When they could not find him later as they traveled back to Nazareth, they were concerned. They hurried back to Jerusalem where they found their son after a three day search. He was in the temple, teaching the elders! Do you remember the exchange between mother and Son?

> *Son, why have You done this to us? Look, your father and I have sought You anxiously.*
> *And He said to them, "Why did you seek Me? Did you not know that I must be about My Father's business?" (Luke 2:48-49)*

Jesus acknowledged the change that had taken place. Though He went back to Nazareth and was subject to His parents after this day, He was not a child any longer. He had to be about His Father's business. They did not understand the clear reference that Jesus was making to His heavenly Father and the mission for which He had been sent to earth. But Joseph and Mary *would* have understood that Jesus had crossed over from childhood to adulthood. The next 18 years of the Savior's life is silent in the Scriptures. We can only assume, because of what people said about Him when He started His ministry, that Jesus learned Joseph's trade and worked as a carpenter during those young adult years.

The child becomes a "young adult" at the age of 12 or 13.

The next time we hear of Jesus in the Scriptures, He is beginning His ministry at the age of 30. We cannot build a doctrine on that, but it is clear from the Scripture that there are young men and there are fathers. John writes in his first epistle to the "little children," the "fathers," and the "young men." There is much agreement that he was addressing men and women in our three stages of life.

Paul said that when he was a child, he spoke, understood, and thought as a child.

...but when I became a man, I put away childish things. (1 Corinthians 13:11).

Paul did not put away childish things and become an "adolescent." That is modern terminology that many use today to excuse the childish behavior of teenagers. Paul left childhood to become a man.

The Greensboro News and Record ran an article on May 3, 2005 entitled, "Kidults reluctant to leave the nest." This front page report coined some new words and phrases like "kidults" and "adultescents," suggesting that research shows the brain of a 17 year old may not be as fully developed as a 30 year old. One sociologist remarked in the article, "If someone insults you at work, an older teen is more likely to throw a punch where an adult would pause and make a sarcastic comment."

I have to confess, neither one of those responses to an insult at work sounds mature, but the reason the 17 year old may throw a punch has less to do with his brain's maturity and more to do with what he has been told and taught since he was born. The message teens hear most often today from school, media, psychology texts and even pulpits is, "You are a child and children behave childishly, and we can't expect you to be anything else."

But that's the wrong message. If the biblical message is that adulthood begins at 12 or 13, then what have we done to our young men and women by continuing to treat them like children, and allowing them to behave that way?

Voddie Baucham, an evangelist in Texas said it like this at the 2005 "Uniting Church and Family Conference" in

Raleigh, NC: "We have taken an army that God has given to the body and said, 'Lay down your arms and go play.'"

Ouch. If Voddie is right, and I believe he is, then the implications for the church and the culture are enormous. We have stunted the growth of the next generation if we tell them they don't have to grow up until they move out. We have handicapped the church if we treat these young warriors like they are second or third string benchwarmers who are not expected to "get in the game" until they get married or finish college. We help the enemy gain ground when we tell these soldiers of 13, 14, 18 that they are to stay behind the lines and keep their powder dry until they get a job and find a life partner. There is a war going on (read Ephesians 6), and we are not just winking at millions of soldiers who are AWOL, we are actually forcing them to run away! They fritter away some of the best and most productive years of their lives when they could be standing shoulder to shoulder with us on the front lines, driving back the spiritual hosts of wickedness. Worst of all, when we deny these young men and women access into the action, the heat of the battle, they grow disillusioned and many end up leaving the faith.

My family visited Boston recently and marveled at the Cradle of Liberty and the men and women who sacrificed to win this country's independence from the British. One of my favorite stories was told to us by a young sailor aboard the USS Constitution. "Old Ironsides," as she was affectionately called, was a frigate in the US Navy, active before and during the War of 1812. She went undefeated against the French and the British, winning 33 battles and losing none. The key, perhaps, to her victories, was the employment of "small boys" and "powder monkeys," as they were called. These were boys and young men, ages 9 to 17. The younger, "small boys" were used to keep water flowing over the loose powder and the hot floor as the big guns were firing. If they were faithful in that task, a boy or young man could become a "powder monkey." These kept the big guns supplied with gunpowder, running below deck to get the powder, running back up to the guns to help load them. The sailor giving us the tour said the USS Constitution could fire 3 rounds in the time it took the British to fire 2, which helped assure our victory and the ship's longevity.

What if the Navy had said, "You boys run and play soldier with sticks and rocks. Come back when you are full-grown men!"

Isn't that what the church has said, in effect, to our young people? "Go play Nintendo, immerse yourself in music and concerts and videos and computer games. Go hang out at the mall. Go dabble in the pleasures of sin for a season. Come back when you get it out of your system and are old enough to serve the church."

What we are doing to these young men, especially, is training them for passivity. Scott Brown said it well at the "Uniting Church and Family Conference" when he stated that "too many men in the church today have PMS."

That got our attention!

Brown continued, "That's 'Passive Male Syndrome.'" I agree. And could it be that *men* are passive many times because they are trained as *youth* to stay out of sight and out of trouble? By the time the church allows them to get involved in the labor of ministry, they are not interested any more. The same principle applies to any kind of work.

My philosophy of teaching my sons to work has always been informed by the knowledge that they will have the desire long before they have the ability! My 6 year old son may want to mow the grass with a push mower, but he is not strong enough. My challenge is to give him responsibility at a young age (2 or 3!) that corresponds to his abilities, and then increase the level of responsibility as his strength and his faithfulness grow. May God give us wisdom as a church to do the same thing with our young men and young women of 12-20.

There are over 130 young people and children aged 18 and younger at Antioch Community Church. More than one-third of those are young adults, 12 years old or older. Here are some ways they are given adult privileges or responsibilities.

- 12 year olds can begin to attend Men's and Women's Retreats.
- 12 year old young men can come to the monthly Men's Breakfast and Bible Study.
- 12 year old young ladies are invited to the annual Women's Christmas Dinner.
- Young men and women are encouraged to prepare to play and sing skillfully and present music for the Sunday morning services.
- Young men and women who are gifted in music and have the heart of a worshiper are invited sometimes to join the worship team on Sundays.
- Young men help receive the offering on Sunday morning.
- Young adults are encouraged to participate in the home group meetings by coming prepared with a testimony of how God is working in their lives that week.
- Young adults are encouraged to discover and use their spiritual gifts to edify the body of Christ.
- Young men are asked to help with meeting physical needs in the body (eg., helping a family move, landscaping a yard for a family in the church, helping an elderly person in the church or community with housecleaning, car repair, yard-work, or whatever is needed).
- We have had a young man (in his teens) running the soundboard at church during the service for the past several years. When one got ready to leave for

college, he trained another young man who was interested in learning.

- My oldest son wanted to invest in the young men at the church, so he asked me about starting a weekly Bible Study for them. He did so, with the help of one of the elders.
- Young people are encouraged to come to church workdays, and they turn out by the dozens. They work hard, doing whatever we give them to do, without complaining!
- Young ladies are called on regularly to assist Moms in the church with childcare or housecleaning or preparing to move.
- Young men and women in the church are treated as adults and asked to be examples *to the believers in word, in conduct, in love, in spirit, in faith, in purity,* (1 Timothy 4:12)

We have Daniels and Josephs and Esthers and Marys and Josiahs and Timothys in our churches. By God's grace, let's train them and encourage them and let them fly toward the target He has prepared for them!

Like arrows in the hand of a warrior, so are the children of one's youth. (Psalm 127:4)

CHAPTER 11

Sheep Need Shepherds!

Another reformation that has taken place at Antioch over the years is the change from a traditional Wednesday night service to mid-week home groups. We started out in 1987 with home groups that met on Wednesday nights and an 'outreach' night on Thursdays at the building. When the church building became available to us on Wednesday nights in the fall of 1988, we discontinued home groups. They would not be revived for about 10 years.

It was the summer of 1998 when we decided it would be a nice change for the summer to meet in a few homes on Wednesday night. We did, and the summer groups were enjoyed by all. When the fall came, however, we went back to business as usual. This went on for a few summers until one day someone said, "Hey, these home groups are great. Why don't we do them all the time? Why do we have to go back to meeting at the building on Wednesday nights during the school year?"

It was one of those moments when one person expressed what was on everybody's heart. The rest of us just didn't know it was on our hearts until he said it!

We have not looked back since. The idea of home groups as a regular part of our life as a church took root and has produced much fruit.

The first thing we did as we realized that the need for groups was outgrowing the number of leaders we had available was set up a training module. The elders talked and prayed and waited until we had a list of men that we believed would be faithful to serve as 'shepherds' of the home groups. Each of those men was approached and asked if he would be willing to serve. If he said "yes," we invited him to join us for a series of meetings where we imparted a vision and a plan for the home groups.

We believed there was ample evidence from the Scriptures that the church has traditionally met together for corporate worship and in smaller groups for teaching, prayer and body life ministry. Paul said to the Ephesian elders that he had proclaimed the full counsel of God to them,

> *and taught (them) publicly and from house to house.*
> *(Acts 20:20)*

We believe that this "public meeting" and this "house to house" meeting represent the two wings of the plane, if you will. Which one is most important? Well, let me ask you. When you fly on an airplane, which wing is most important to you?

I don't get on a plane unless it has both firmly in place!

It is the purpose of the church on Sunday morning to come together to exalt God in corporate worship. The meeting is a celebration of Him. We believe that Sunday morning ought to be a place where our hearts and our eyes are on the King of Kings and the Lord of Lords. He is worthy of our deepest devotion and our loudest praise. We want to sing and preach and pray and give and testify with exultation on Sunday morning. If sinners or seekers come, praise God, they will see how much we love Him and that He is the center of our joy! But we do not tailor the service in any way to appeal to or to appease the seeker. We lift up the name of Jesus and exalt that name which is above every name. The people are challenged with Christ-exalting messages, and Sunday morning is vertical in its orientation.

The mid-week service is the other wing of the plane. It is a time to love the body of Christ through fellowship, through the "one-anothers" of Scripture. We encourage one another, we pray for one another, we minister to one another. It is at the home group that believers can "try out" a ministry, if they believe they have a gift of teaching, for example. There is usually praise music at these meetings, but not always. There is most definitely a focus on prayer and the Word in the context of a body life service in someone's living room.

Each group is led by two or three men. These are men that have been selected by the elders because their spiritual and physical houses are in order, and they have a vision and a desire to help shepherd the flock. We call them "shepherds," and they are asked to take responsibility for the people that are placed in their home groups by praying for them, leading the meetings, protecting their 'flock' from false teaching or anything that would be out of order, and by preparing spiritual food from God's Word to feed their flock each week.

Most of the time we try to place an older man and a younger man together as shepherds so that discipleship can take place in the leadership team as well as in the small group. We ask the Holy Spirit to direct us, and we have been amazed at the number of times He has put two men together who perfectly complement each other with their different personalities and gift-mixes.

The shepherds are free to lead their sheep into any pasture of God's Word that they like. There have been small groups who studied the Gospels, the book of Acts, the Proverbs, Romans, Philippians, and more. There are also times when a small group will go through a Bible Study together, such as the series produced by "Focus on the Family" entitled, "That the World May Know." Sometimes the elders will *encourage* the shepherds to study a particular passage or go through a particular book, but so far this has been the exception rather than the rule. We want the shepherds to be able to discern for themselves what the Lord is saying about their particular group, and we ask them to

> *Be diligent to know the state of your flocks, and attend to your herds (Proverbs 27:23).*

Each group comes up with its own plan for taking care of the little ones. The groups meet together, there is no age-segregation, but they are free to provide childcare for the children under two years old, if need be. For example, in the group I am currently helping to shepherd, we have a couple of little girls who are under two years old. Most of the time they are quite content to sit and play or color in the middle of the floor. But then there are times when all they want to do is fuss or squeal or run through the house. There are two ways we can go, when this is the case.

One, either Mom or Dad will have to pick up the little one and walk with her in the kitchen, or, if that doesn't keep her quiet enough so the others can hear each other, they will walk in the yard. Of course, the goal is to train the child to sit and listen, so we encourage Dads and Moms to stay close by with the child to be able to participate in the discussion and ministry. The second way we have dealt with children on occasion is to ask my 16 year old daughter, or another young lady in the group, if she would mind taking the little ones upstairs to play, where their fussing will not disturb the others. I realize that doing that takes my daughter out of the room for 30-45 minutes, while the rest of us have Bible Study and prayer time. But it frees up that Mom or that Dad who came in frazzled and needing to be encouraged by adults. Again, the emphasis for each shepherd is this: *you* decide what will work best for your group.

Once every 6 weeks or so, we will meet together as a church on Wednesday night. The reason we do that is three-fold. First, we want to give the host families a break. It is a difficult thing to have 12-30 people (or even more!) show up at your doorstep every Wednesday night, and we know this gives them a breather and helps prevent burnout. Second, we love to be together as a church, and that Wednesday night once every 6 weeks provides another time when we can catch up with each other, especially the people who are *not* in our home group! Third, that Wednesday night has been a great time to hear from a missionary, to enjoy a song that some of the youth have prepared, to have a 'business meeting' of sorts and let the elders share something with the church to help re-direct our vision or speak to a potential problem before it develops any further, or just to get in small groups and pray all over the room for a member of our church family who is very sick. We have even gone to a local park on those Wednesday nights to have pizza and play volleyball and be a witness to the community.

The home groups change every year in September. There are two reasons why the elders ask the people to go to a different group every year. The first reason is so the people can get to know others in the church. The small groups, hopefully, develop a chemistry in the early months of their time together. By the time they are ready to divide and join other groups, they have learned to share their hearts with one another and be open and honest about their own struggles. That is a good thing! It glorifies God when we obey His Word that tells us to

Confess your trespasses to one another, and pray for one another, that you may be healed. The effec-

tive, fervent prayer of a righteous man avails much. (James 5:16).

The more people in the church we have that kind of a relationship with, the stronger the church and the greater the witness to the community, which results in greater glory to God.

The second reason we ask the people to change groups is because some of them never would. In fact, if left to themselves, some groups would face a strong temptation to split from the church and start another congregation. It has happened in many churches, as some of you well know. To help prevent this type of insular thinking from even getting a chance to incubate in any one group, we ask the people to join a different group every September. However, we also give them this instruction with an option: "Pray and seek the Lord about His will for you concerning this next year's home group. If you believe the Lord is telling you to stay where you are (assuming a particular shepherd is going to host a group in his home again, for example), then you may certainly do that."

This happens sometimes. There may be a young family, for example, who has been particularly blessed by one of the shepherds in the church. That man and his wife have loved this young couple and really taken them under their wings, and now it is time to change groups, but both couples believe their time together is not yet complete. They are free to stay together for a second year. But there will need to be a change for the third year.

The shepherds meet with the elders once a month for prayer and discussion. It usually falls on the third Sunday of the month, when we have Men's Breakfast for all the men and young men of the church from 7:45-9:15.

The shepherds and the elders will meet at 6:45 am for an hour, and I will open with a short word of devotion, something I believe will encourage and instruct the shepherds in their ministry. This will often lead to a discussion about the passage I read from, and it is a wonderful time when,

> *As iron sharpens iron, so a man sharpens the countenance of his friend.* (Proverbs 27:17).

That is followed by a time of sharing, around the table, about what is happening in each home group. If there is a concern one of the shepherds has that can be discussed freely in the meeting, he will bring it to the table for the elders to discuss, and the other men can participate as well. There are sometimes questions about helping parents deal with child discipline, or about someone who has missed meetings and needs our prayers and encouragement.

This monthly meeting may also be a time for vision casting, when I or one of the other elders will exhort the brothers in our responsibility to take care of the flock. For example, when one of the ladies at Antioch has a baby, we as a church like to provide two weeks of meals, delivered to her house by different families. If possible, a member of the home group which this lady and her husband attend will oversee the administration of those meals. Or, if there is a problem in the home group, the elders encourage the shepherds to be the first line of defense, to try and resolve the problem if they can. If the elders need to be called to help give counsel, then that happens after the shepherds have given their attention and prayer to the matter first. (This is wonderful 'on-the-job' training for future elders!)

When people visit our church, one of the first things they might say to me or someone else about Antioch is, "Where did you find all of these men of God who love the Word and who take responsibility to lead the church?" The answer is, we didn't find them. Most likely, they didn't come to Antioch that way, although some did. Most of the men grew up here (me included!) as we were given opportunity to minister and to lead and as we were challenged by the examples we see all around us to be a man of faith and a man of the Word. It is a very exciting and a very biblical thing to behold, and God alone gets the credit.

I would add that these men who serve the church by exercising leadership are supported by wives who love them and respect the calling that is on their lives. I know very well the sacrifice that is required for a man to be a leader in the church. And that sacrifice is not just made by him, but by his wife and his children as well. If the men are meeting for prayer and Bible Study on Sunday mornings once a month, then that leaves their wives to take care of things on the home-front by themselves. The enemy loves to target that time and stir strife in the marriage and even cause bitterness and resentment if he can. It takes two to make a church leader: a man who knows he is called and will do the work of a leader while not neglecting his primary duties as a husband and father, and a woman who will pay the extra price behind the scenes so that her husband can serve the body of Christ. When both husband and wife work together as a ministry team in that way, it is glorious and Christ-honoring.

When a man has proven himself faithful as a shepherd, we may ask him to go through training to become an elder....

CHAPTER 12

What's the Big Deal about Elders?

The Chicago Sun-Times carried this story on July 11, 2005.

ISTANBUL, Turkey – "First one sheep jumped to its death. Then stunned Turkish shepherds, who had left the herd to graze while they had breakfast, watched as nearly 1,500 others followed, each leaping off the same cliff, Turkish media reported.

In the end, 450 dead animals lay on top of one another in a billowy white pile, the Aksam newspaper said. Those who jumped later were saved as the pile got higher and the fall more cushioned.

After one of the sheep tried to jump a ravine, the rest of the flock followed.

'There's nothing we can do. They're all wasted,' Nevzat Bayhan, a member of one of 26 families whose sheep were grazing in the herd, was quoted as saying…" *AP*

What is going on here? You have heard the mythical story, perhaps, of lemmings rushing to the sea, committing suicide en masse. Here we have a similar story, only this time it is a herd of sheep, all following a leader who is very confused.

This rogue sheep made a deadly decision and 1,500 of his closest friends blindly followed him.

You could "spin" this story and say that 450 of the sheep laid down their lives for their comrades. But don't pull the wool over your eyes. That's not what happened here.

You could say that sheep are naturally sociable and would rather die together than live alone. That, too, would be wrong, and I would be fleecing you to even suggest it.

You could say that since these were sheep in Turkey, perhaps they thought they could fly. That would be a really "baaad" attempt at humor, and it, too, would be off the mark.

No, these sheep were simply acting the way God designed them. Sheep are not the brightest of four-legged creatures, they are defenseless, and they do tend to be followers. Hence, sheep desperately need a shepherd.

Maybe that's why God compares us to sheep in the Bible. He says in Isaiah 53:6,

> *"All we like sheep have gone astray; we have turned, every one, to his own way..."*

Sheep, if left unattended, will wander off. A sheep can wander over a cliff, or into a thicket where he is held fast, or stumble over rocks and end up 'cast' (on his back, unable to turn). In any of these scenarios, the sheep that leaves his shepherd is easy prey for a wolf, a hyena, or any number of sheep-eating predators.

"Prone to wander, Lord I feel it, prone to leave the God I love."

But this story from Turkey also illustrates the need for the shepherd to stay with the sheep. Maybe that is why Jesus said of himself,

> *"I am the good shepherd. The good shepherd gives his life for the sheep." (John 10:11)*

Sheep need a faithful shepherd. We have one, the only one, in Jesus.

It was Jesus Christ, the Son of God, who was visited in Bethlehem by poor shepherds who had heard the news from angels of the Savior's birth. It was Jesus Christ, the Lamb of God, who gave up his own life on the cross in exchange for mine and for yours. It is Jesus Christ, the conquering King, who will return one day to separate the sheep from the goats, to gather those who have believed His word and had their sins washed away by His blood.

This writer is one sheep who is keeping his eye, by God's grace, on the Shepherd.

If there is one lesson I have learned about the church in the past eighteen years as a pastor, it is this one: there is not much that is more important to a church's vitality and even its survival than healthy, vibrant, maturing leadership. Leadership in a church is a wonderful thing and desperately needed. But sometimes that fact is not appreciated, by the elders *or* by the people who are supposed to follow them. Let me illustrate with the following story.

A few years ago, I took one of my sons to Liberty University to compete in a national speech and debate tournament. I had some free time one afternoon, so I was sitting on the top landing of the DeMoss Learning Center, the center building of campus, an imposing structure with huge columns and many steps leading up to the landing and the front doors. There were two groups of boys on that landing playing four-square, using basketballs. And they were kind of a nuisance because the balls would get loose and hit people trying to enter the building, or go flying down the steps, threatening to bowl someone over who was coming up. I was watching this, wondering, *Where are their parents?*, when the man in charge of the debate tournament walked up the steps and saw what was going on. We had been introduced to this man at the opening convocation and were told that he is the head of

Debate at Liberty University, so I knew he had authority in this setting.

He said, firmly, "Boys, don't play ball up here." Then he said it again before he entered the DeMoss building. Well, the reaction to his directive was interesting. Out of the 10-15 boys playing four-square, I believe there were *two* who wanted to comply and said to the others, "Come on, guys, let's go find another place to play."

But they were met with protests all around by young boys aspiring to be Philadelphia lawyers.

"No! This is the best place!" "Why should we leave?" "Yeah, who was HE anyway? He's just a parent!" "That's right, he's just a parent. He can't tell us not to play up here!"

Hey, what was I supposed to do? I couldn't just sit there and let this happen, could I?!

I said, "Excuse me, boys, but that was Mr. Smith (not his real name), the head of Debate at Liberty University. He *can* tell you not to play here."

That started a buzz as they discussed whether they were going to believe me or not. They walked away from me on the landing, still arguing. They were in a quandary. Now they had *two* people telling them they had to stop doing what they wanted to do. How would they respond? I went back to reading my book, thinking it was over and these boys would just wander off to find another place to play. Then I looked up to see two of them standing in front of me.

The ringleader spoke: "I've seen the guy you're talking about, Mr. Smith, and that's not him."

He said it with as much confidence as he could muster, but I could see that he wasn't really sure of his facts. I smiled and said, "That *is* him. Trust me." Then I added, again with a smile, "But if *any* adult told you to stop playing ball up here, you ought to stop."

The other boy weighed in: "But we've been playing here for 2 days!"

I said, "It doesn't matter how long you've been playing. If an adult asks you to stop, you should obey." I could see resignation in the boys' eyes.

Then the ring leader said, "Should we go tell *those* guys?" (pointing to the group that was on the far side of the landing).

"You should!" I said. "Spread the word!"

Now, let's look at this story and see what was going on with these boys. And let's put each of their arguments in the context of the church and the biblical leadership God has ordained in His Word, the leadership provided by elders.

Think about this story of the boys playing four-square. What was their first argument? "He doesn't have authority over us." Remember their first statement? "He's just a parent, he can't tell us what to do." What the boys were really saying, and wanting to believe, was that they were not under authority, that they could do whatever they wanted to do, and besides, they weren't hurting anybody, they were just playing four-square!

I have heard the same argument made by adults, in reaction to a decision by the elders. "Hey, who do those guys think they are? They can't tell *me* what to do!"

My first response, then, is simple.
The New Testament model for leadership is a council of elders.

That's why Paul said to Titus,

For this reason I left you in Crete, that you should set in order the things that are lacking, and appoint elders in every city as I commanded you— (Titus 1:5).

That's why Luke tells us that Paul and Barnabus

appointed elders in every church, and prayed with fasting, (and) they commended them to the Lord in whom they had believed. (Acts 14:23).

That's why Paul spends a great deal of time in 1 Timothy 3 and Titus 1 going over the qualifications for an elder. That's why Peter exhorted the elders to

> *Shepherd the flock of God which is among you...*
> *(1 Peter 5:2).*

That's why Paul entreated the Ephesian elders at Miletus to

> *take heed to yourselves and to all the flock, among*
> *which the Holy Spirit has made you overseers, to*
> *shepherd the church of God which He purchased*
> *with His own blood. (Acts 20:28).*

In each of these passages, we see the same thing. God has ordained a biblical model for church leadership, a council of elders. And I would submit to you that healthy, vital churches that are achieving what God has called them to, without exception have healthy, vital leadership.

What are elders? Your translation may say bishop, or overseer, or shepherd. But it's the same thing. The Jews preferred the term, ***presbuteros,*** which means mature, dignified, wise, even "gray-haired." The Greeks preferred the word ***episkopos***, and that means "overseer" or one who takes responsibility. But they are used interchangeably in the New Testament because elders must be both: mature believers who lead the flock and take care of them. One word denotes the dignity of the office and the other word denotes the duties.

So, let's go back to the boys playing four-square. Their first argument was, "He doesn't have authority over us." And they were wrong. Our God is a God of order, not of chaos. He has not set up a random universe that operates whimsically, but an ordered universe that works according to laws that He has ordained. And as the saying goes, you don't *break* the law of gravity by jumping off a 10 story building. You break *yourself* against it. God's order for church leadership is clear. He has spoken clearly in His Word that the church has authority in place, the council of elders.

Let's look at the *second* statement the boys made. It was, "That's not the RIGHT authority figure!" It was really a smokescreen, they didn't want to obey ANY authority if they could get away with it, but we can make an analogy between this statement by the boys and the typical church-goer in America who has bought into the corporate model of pastoral leadership. But the Word is clear...

The New Testament model for church leadership is a *council* of elders.

As "Herman's Hermits" used to sing, "Second verse, same as the first." It's the same point again, I realize, but the em*phas*is is on a different sy*llab*le. Notice the New Testament model is a PLURALITY of elders, not a single pastor. This is something I have said repeatedly from the pulpit for 18 years, but I believe it bears repeating over and over until we get it.

So many of us grew up in churches with solo leadership that it is part of our ecclesiology and very difficult to shake. We think the church ought to operate like a corporation: one person at the top, the CEO, and everybody else is under him. Or, there is a board of elders or a board of deacons, or a consistory, or whatever terminology we want to call it, but it is still a hierarchy, and one man (or in some churches, one woman) has final authority and can overrule all the rest.

That's what those boys were saying, in essence: he's not Mr. Smith, he's just one of his lackeys who has no authority.

How does that relate to church members in the 21st century? How many times are people offended if when they are sick, the *pastor* doesn't call or visit. Instead, they get a call from Bertha, a sweet lady in the church, and a visit from one of the men who leads their home group, and cards from half a dozen people. But none of that matters, because the *pastor* didn't visit! That's a corporate model-understanding of church leadership, *not* a biblical understanding!

Or how many get nervous if someone besides the *pastor* is preaching. Or, maybe they don't even show up that day unless "the man of God" is in the pulpit! Aren't the elders men of God who are able to teach? They should be!

Remember all the verses we just looked at? Peter exhorted the *elders* to shepherd the flock. Paul instructed Titus to appoint *elders*. When Paul was on his way to Jerusalem, he didn't call for the *pastor* of the church at Ephesus, but he called for the *elders*.

Perhaps one of the most telling verses of all is found in Acts 14:23:

So when they had appointed elders in every church...

Paul and Barnabas, the first church planters appointed *elders* (plural) in *every church* (singular)!

The church is to be led by a plurality of elders, and this was a unique, Holy Spirit-led creation of a new form of government. It wasn't anything like the way the world set up leadership models. And it wasn't anything like the way the Jews had set up leadership models. It was a new wineskin, and it was just right for the new wine of life in Jesus Christ!

Now, there is another concept that was at work in the New Testament that we practice here at Antioch. The Romans called it *primus inter pares*, which means, "first among equals." And I believe the Bible clearly teaches what Alexander Strauch writes in his book, <u>Biblical Eldership</u>: "Although elders act jointly as a council and share equal authority and responsibility for the leadership of the church, all are not equal in their giftedness, biblical knowledge, leadership ability, experience or dedication."

The concept of *first among equals* can be seen throughout Scripture. Peter was the leader of the disciples. He had no more authority than any one of the 12, but they seemed to follow his lead. It was James, the brother of Jesus, who was the leader of the church in Jerusalem. He was the one who made the final decision after the discussion and debate regarding requirements for Gentile believers in Acts 15. (see Acts 15:13-21) It was Paul who emerged as the leader of the Paul and Barnabus missionary team, though it started off the other way around.

One man will emerge as the leader, as the *first among equals*, in the council of elders.

So, though I am called "pastor" at Antioch, and I believe I am functioning in the role as pastor/teacher because of my particular giftings and callings, I have no more authority here than the other elders. I may be the "first among equals," but that doesn't give me two votes on any decision!

Also, the "first among equals" role changes according to what we are doing. When we are discussing financial matters, there is one elder in particular we expect to take the lead in helping to make that decision. When we are discussing difficult passages of Scripture and trying to understand what the whole council of the Word is when it comes to a particular doctrine, there is another elder besides myself who will often take the lead in helping to make that decision. So, even though it looks like most of time I am the *mouth* (like Peter was for the disciples), I am not the only one who leads. Jesus Christ is our head, and He works through a plurality of elders to lead Antioch Church. And I am so thankful for the men He has raised up to take care of this church that He bought with His own blood. To God be the glory!

Let's look at the next statement the boys made. It was, "We've been playing here for two days!" Translated, they were saying several things:

1. We like this, it's fun, it's comfortable for us, so leave us alone.

2. We have ALWAYS done it this way, and we are
   not going to change now!
3. If we can think of a reason NOT to obey, then we
   don't have to obey. Besides, his command didn't
   make sense to us!

Here is my response, tried and true though it may be.

The New Testament model for church **leadership** is a council of elders.

OK, I know you think I'm messing with you, now, but again, it's the same point, only with a different emphasis.

The Bible compares the people of God most often to.... sheep. That's right. And what do sheep need more than anything else? That's right, a shepherd. Healthy sheep are healthy sheep because they have a good shepherd. The shepherd does for the sheep what good elders will do for the church: Elders are charged to protect the flock, to feed the flock, to lead the flock, and to care for the flock. Those are all GOOD things, things we all need! So, it stands to reason that the New Testament model for church leadership is something that will benefit the church and all the people who are a part of it.

The boys said, "We like this, it's fun!" People need leadership much more than they need comfort or entertainment. A sheep that is comfortable and ignores the call of the shepherd ends up being devoured by wolves. It is the same with the people of God, as Paul said to the Ephesian elders in Acts 20.

The boys said, "We have always done it this way!" People need leadership much more than they need their traditions. That was Jesus' basic message to the religious leaders of His day: Leave your traditions and come and follow Me. Freedom is not license to do what I want to do but liberty to do what I ought to do. God gives to the church *leaders* who will model that principle, teach that principle, and enforce that principle.

The boys said, "We can think of lots of reason not to obey. And besides, the command makes no sense to us."

Churches in our postmodern culture today are filled with people who would answer this way. They might say to the elders, "It makes no sense to us that you want our family to be a part of a home group. Until we understand it with our mind or until we feel it with our heart, we will continue to do what we want to do rather than what you are asking us to do."

I believe one of the most important questions in life is this one: "Who, or what, is the source of authority in your life?"

In other words, why do you live the way you live? I would contend that everything we do is based on something we believe. If I jump in the car to ride 2 miles to see a friend, and do not buckle my seat belt, then what belief supports my action? It is the belief that I will not have an accident, and if I do, I will be safe without my seat belt securely fastened. Can we agree that basing my action on what I think to be true is not always the best policy, and may even cost me my life?

Nevertheless, there are many who live according to their intellect, according to what they can reason out in their minds, even about the Scriptures. Like those boys, they say, "I will obey it if it makes sense to me, unless I can rationalize a reason *not* to obey!

Then there are others (by far the largest group) who live according to what they feel.

Ray Comfort tells the story of two women from California who were about to cross the Mexican border to go back to the U.S. As they approached the border, they saw what looked like a very small dog, shivering in the ditch beside the road. They stopped the car and got out to look at the animal, and as they examined it in the darkness, they thought it was a tiny Chihuahua. Their hearts were immediately broken by the plight of this poor animal and then and there they decided, based on what their hearts were saying, to take it over the border and back home. They determined to rescue this poor critter and nurse it back to health. However, because they were afraid that they might be breaking the law, they put it in the trunk of their car until they got across the border.

Once they were clear of the border guards, they pulled over, took the animal from the trunk and let it lay between them on the front seat of the car. When they arrived back in their home town, one of the ladies took the animal home because it was too late to go to the vet. That night it slept beside her in the bed, and during the night she woke up several times and reached over to comfort the ailing creature. It was so sick the next morning that she decided to take it first thing to the vet. That's when she found out that the animal wasn't a tiny sick dog.

It was a Mexican water rat, dying of rabies.

What's wrong with living by how I feel? *That's* what's wrong with living by how I feel! My heart can be a liar. God said to the prophet Jeremiah,

> **The heart is deceitful above all things, and desper-**
> **ately wicked; who can know it? (17:9).**

If I cannot trust what I think because my intellect is flawed, and I cannot trust what I feel because my heart can deceive me, what do I do? I thought you'd never ask! In John 5, Jesus rebukes the Jews who searched the Scriptures for intellectual reasons, not because they were looking for truth, saying to them:

> **But you are not willing to come to Me that you may**
> **have life. (John 5:40).**

The source of authority is Jesus Christ Himself, and He requires that we lay our intellect and our feelings at His feet. He will restore them when we come to Him by faith, and He will give us life.

The boys at Liberty were using their intellect and their emotions in the wrong way. Instead of submitting to authority with gladness and rejoicing, they were trying to use their thoughts and their feelings to somehow get around authority. How many in the church today do the same thing?

That's why God called the church fathers to appoint elders.

But if you agree with my premise that Scripture is clear with regard to elders leading the church, that begs the question: where do those elders come from, especially in a brand new church?

I get calls regularly from men who are involved in starting a family-integrated church, and one of the questions I hear most often has to do with leadership. This is one that came last week:

"Matthew and I are serving as provisional elders. Here's my question; what should be the process for establishing permanent elders? When is the appropriate time?"

That's a great question! It speaks to me of a man who is not willing to adopt the corporate model and impose it on the church, but wants to be faithful to what the Word teaches regarding church leadership. Here's how I responded:

In my experience it is MUCH to be preferred to have no elders than to have the wrong elders. If you and Matthew are able to handle the shepherding duties at this time, then my counsel would be to take your time in appointing other elders, lay hands quickly on no man. I would seek the Lord about the men in the congregation that you believe are elder material, and then take them through a training process. In my opinion, three things need to line up before a man is appointed as an elder. First, he must have the desire (1 Tim. 3:1). He must not be serving under compulsion but willingly (1 Peter 5). Second, he must have the qualifications (1 Tim. 3, Titus 1, 1 Peter 5, Acts 20, etc). Obviously, he will not have perfected any of them, but his "progress will be evident to all" (1 Tim. 4:15) Third, it must be the right time. (For example, if he is a novice, he certainly should not become an elder. But what if he is a 'novice' to the church? I believe the man who would serve as an elder must spend time getting to know and to love the flock that he will be helping to shepherd. Therefore, if Doug Phillips (of "Vision Forum") came and joined our church next week, we would not make him an elder the following week, even though he obviously is an elder in the church. We would want to wait until he knew and loved "the flock that is among" us (1 Peter 5).

If any one of those three qualifications is not there, my counsel is to wait until it is. You don't want to "marry (your-self to another elder) in haste and repent in leisure."

A few days after I responded to the question, which had been addressed to three men from three different churches in three different areas of North Carolina, this response was emailed by another of the men:

I heartily concur with what my brothers have written below, especially the belief that it is "better to have no elders than the wrong elders." And, based on Tit. 1:9ff, I would add <u>the necessity of elders being like-minded in all signifi-cant doctrine and practice</u> (though admittedly we will not be in perfect agreement this side of heaven). Otherwise, how will the elders teach sound doctrine and refute error? How will they avoid leaving confusion among the flock when the "error" that one elder is refuting is the "sound doctrine" of another elder? (John Thompson)

Amen! If the elders disagree about what "sound doctrine" is, there will be the inevitable 'divorce' among the elders, resulting in suffering for the entire fellowship. There must be a significant amount of time devoted to the training and preparation of a potential elder.

I could say a lot more here about the training process and the qualifications a man must have before he becomes an elder. But I cannot say it any better than it has been said by Paul and Peter in the New Testament. And I could not explain those Scriptures any better than I believe Alexander Strauch has, in his book <u>Biblical Eldership</u>. (Lewis & Roth, 1995)

What we have done at Antioch is watch the men of the church to see who is already doing the work of an elder *without* the title. Is there a brother who has a burden to disciple other men? Is there a brother who comes forward to pray for someone during the service when the opportunity arises? Is there a brother who is hungering after the Lord and is attentive to the Word and is faithful to teach other faithful men, as 2 Timothy 2:2 requires? Is there a brother who is managing his own household well, who loves his wife and is training up faithful and disciplined children? Who is the brother who has a solid reputation among unbelievers and has his financial house in order? This is probably a man who is already doing the work of an elder!

We will ask that man (or men) to go through a training process that lasts up to 6 months or more. I ask them to read several books (including <u>Biblical Eldership</u> by Strauch) and meet with me (or with all the elders who are able) once a month to discuss what they have read. The men go through a time of searching the Scriptures and asking the Lord to search their own hearts. If at the end of that process they believe they are ready, the elders will meet with them to discuss the church's doctrine, vision, and philosophy of ministry, and to examine their walk with the Lord and their reputation with outsiders. The next step is to go before the congregation and ask the body to pray for these potential elders, and for us as we ask the Lord for wisdom. We ask the body to let us know if they have any concerns about these men becoming elders. At the end of 30 days or so, there being no objections of merit, we will bring the men before the congregation at the end of a Sunday morning service and pray for them with the laying on of hands. They become elders that day and will continue to serve as long as they are able. There have been elders who, after serving for a year or two, have asked to step aside because they are involved in an itinerant ministry, for example, that prevents them from giving the work of an elder what it requires. But I praise God that He has been faithful to bring in and raise up godly men who can serve.

As I am writing this book, I am blessed to have so many men in the church who are gifted and capable of rightly dividing the Word of truth. During the months of July and August in the summer of 2005, I preached only twice in 9 weeks, so that I could devote a significant amount of time each day writing this book. The other seven Sundays were handled by the other two elders, by two men who are training to be elders, and by three men who are shepherds.

The church did not suffer in the least with me out of the pulpit for a while!

CHAPTER 13

Preference or Principle?

Yes, it's true. A family-integrated church can have problems. I have figured out a way, though, to eliminate all
the problems in the church. All of them. You ready for this?

Get rid of all the people.

That's right. As long as there is one person in the church,
there will be conflict. You have heard the story of the man,
perhaps, who was stranded by himself on a deserted island
for seven years. When he was finally found, he showed his
rescuers around the island. They noticed he had built three huts
for himself, and asked him what they were for.

"This one is where I live," he said, pointing to the first hut.
"This one is where I go to church," pointing to the third hut.

"What's the other hut for?" the rescuers asked.

"That's where I *used* to go to church."

That's the sad truth. Even if the church consisted of you
all by yourself, there would be conflict. So, how do we deal
with it?

There have been books, even series of books, written about
dealing with church conflict. I do not presume to know anything
that anyone who has written about the subject doesn't know.

But I can tell you from my experience, and from the Bible, that conflict in any church is inevitable.

The first church was rocking along pretty smoothly until Ananias and Sapphira decided to lie to the apostles about their offering. You can read about it Acts 5, but the conflict between leadership and members was short, but not sweet. They lied and they died. End of story.

I would like to say that the conflict we have had at Antioch has been dealt with that quickly (if not that dramatically!), but it hasn't.

The second time we see conflict in the early church happened right after Ananias and Sapphira caught a red-eye out of there.

You can read about it in Chapter 6 of Acts, and the problem occurred because the Grecian widows in the church were being overlooked in the daily distribution of food. Was it racially motivated? Maybe so, but nonetheless the apostles dealt with it swiftly and decisively. They asked the church to select seven men who were full of the Holy Spirit and wisdom. These men were recommended to the elders who then appointed them as the first deacons in the church.

I wish I could say that every time we have had a conflict in the church, the elders have wisely done what the first church leaders did: discern the heart issues, allowed the Holy Spirit to speak and to act, and appointed godly men who could address the problem and solve it. That has not always been the case, but we have learned a few things about dealing with conflict.

First, I believe the Lord has taught us that much conflict comes when people have a different vision or philosophy of ministry. At the core of these conflicts is a difference in principle.

We lost a number of families all at once a few years ago who left to start a house church. They wanted a worship service on Sunday morning that was unstructured and "free."

They didn't want anyone among them to be called "pastor," lest he be elevated above them in his own mind or in theirs. They wanted each of the cell groups to be churches in their own right, and some even suggested that we not meet but once a month or so all together, and meet weekly in small groups.

I understand that there is a "cell-based church" model that is being used out there, and that's fine. But the elders at this local church don't happen to agree with some of the philosophy of ministry that cell-based churches embrace. We differ in principle.

So, the elders met with the men of these families, and we looked at the issues they were raising. We looked at the Scriptures together. We talked about our differences of opinion, we discussed, and sometimes we debated. In the end, we had to come to them and say, "We do not agree with this vision you are proposing for Antioch. We would like for you to stay with us and be a part of what God is doing here, but if you cannot agree with our direction as a church, it would be better for all concerned if you leave."

Amos 3:3 says,

Can two walk together unless they are agreed?

I like the way Doug Phillips explained it at the "Uniting Church and Family" Conference in 2003, and this is a paraphrase. He said that if we are 'walking together' at a conference, for example, we can disagree about a lot of doctrinal or ministry issues, and it really doesn't matter. Jesus is Lord, and we agree on that. If, however, we are going to work together on a ministry project or be employed together in the same ministry, there are fewer issues and doctrines upon which we can disagree. We need to walk more closely together if we yoke ourselves in ministry. But if we are going to get *married*, then we must really make sure that we are walking together!

In the case of the house church brethren, we realized that we had a different vision and could no longer walk together in the same fellowship. We can certainly walk together in the same community and we can share ministry, eat together, enjoy fellowship, and we must do that for the sake of unity in the body of Christ. But we do not have to be in the same local church fellowship, and in fact, to try and make it work when we are pulling in two different directions would just be misery for all concerned.

We have also had conflict in the church over issues that I considered more "preference" than principle. One of those is the style of music we use on Sunday mornings.

It is the elders' strong belief at Antioch that when Paul said in Ephesians we are to speak

> *to one another in psalms and hymns and spiritual songs, singing and making melody in your heart to the Lord (Ephesians 5:19),*

Paul is saying the heart of worship is the worship of the heart. God is delighted with worship that is reflective of a heart directed toward Him. We worship Him from a heart that is satisfied with Him, delighted in Him. As John Piper says, "God is most glorified in us when we are most satisfied in Him" (Desiring God, p.10), and that is a heart issue. Is God my delight? Then when I worship Him with song, it matters not whether I sing a hymn or a chorus or a psalm! What God sees is my heart that is turned toward Him. David said,

> *The Lord is my strength and my shield; my heart trusted in Him, and I am helped; therefore my heart greatly rejoices, and with my song I will praise Him. (Psalm 28:7)*

John Piper addressed this in a sermon entitled "Worship That Comes By the Word" in 2002. He says:

"If you don't like (contemporary) worship songs, be careful that you don't get caught up in comparing the worst worship songs with the best hymns. It's not fair! Compare the best worship songs with the best hymns and the worst worship songs with the worst hymns, because there are a lot of lousy hymns, just like there are a lot of lousy worship songs. So be fair in your comparison and your critique of what's happening in worship. But in the best worship songs, two things are happening: The mind is being brought, with God-centered lyrics, in an amazing way, into engagement with God. And the heart, stirred by these contemporary tunes, is being engaged, with tenderness, devotion, enjoyment...at least for millions of people this is true, even if not for a lot of musical classicists. So, I look at this and I am amazed at what has happened, the God-centeredness of contemporary worship songs. God is exalted, He is Lord, He is risen from the dead, He's majestic, He's mighty, He's holy. He has conquered the power of death, He's a shield, He's glory, He's the lifter of our heads, He's great, He's wonderful, He's rock, He's fortress, He's deliverer. He's the coming King, He's the redeemer, name above all names, Messiah, Lamb of God, Holy One, He is God, and Our God Reigns!...It's an amazing thing that has happened in the lyrics of popular worship music. If you don't like the drums, if you don't like the guitars, if you don't like electricity...if you don't like all of that, you still have to admit that by and large the lyrics of this phenomenon are God-ward. They are almost pure Scripture again and again and again, even if sometimes clumsily set to the music. And the hoped-for effect is a relentless addressing of God directly for the engagement of the heart."

Amen!

At Antioch we want to be faithful to keep the good hymns alive, for they are powerful and deep. We also want to be able to sing the older choruses, *and* learn the new ones that are biblically sound. In other words, we attempt a blended style of worship music, and sometimes we succeed and sometimes we fail.

If someone comes into the church and is convinced that it is a Scriptural principle that only hymns should be sung by church people, they will be frustrated at Antioch, and may leave. Some have done so. Or if someone comes in and believes that since he was weaned on "Relient K" and raised on "Switchfoot," we need a light show on Sunday mornings and maybe even a mosh pit, he will *definitely* be disappointed. It's not going to happen.

But again, the issue of music is a preference at Antioch, not a principle. If you go to a church and the preferences are different, I believe you should submit your preferences to the Lord and throw yourself into the church as a servant. If you do anything else, it will ultimately lead to conflict. For example, if I went to a church and really hated the color of the sanctuary carpet, I can either close my eyes and raise my hands and worship God...or I can start a whisper campaign in the church that *something* has to be done about the carpet.

If I select door number one, I will probably find myself growing closer to the Lord, respecting the elders and their authority, and inviting others to my church. And pretty soon, I won't even SEE the carpet! If I select door number two, I will be miserable, the people I speak to will be miserable, the elders will have pressure put on them that they never should have had to deal with, and I will be disobedient to the Word of God because He told me not to let anything come out of my mouth except that which will

impart grace to the hearers (Ephesians 4:29).

If you absolutely cannot stand it and have to tell someone, first tell the Lord. Cry out to Him about the carpet or the music or the nursery or the Bible translation that is used or whether the ushers smile or frown when they take up the offering or the women's ministry or the men's ministry or (you fill in the blank) _____.

Give that some time. Read the Word and pray. You may even want to fast. The Lord delivers sometimes only through prayer *and* fasting, and He may want to deliver you!

If after 3 months you are still upset, go talk to someone. Go talk to the elders if your concern is something that the elders decided and only the elders can change. Take your concern to them and to them only. Go respectfully, without accusation and without complaining.

Here's the way one person wrote about this issue on an email loop:

> I believe too many of us tend to have a Pharisaical spirit that elevates issues of practice and preference to the level of essential doctrine. Many Christians reject a church (or their fellow Christians) because of "mint and cumin" issues, while neglecting the weightier issues of the heart that our Lord spoke of. If the enemy of our souls can't defeat us with worldliness and distraction he will use spiritual pride as an evil wedge to divide Christians and churches. It's a real and present danger for all of us. (Victoria A. Schellhase, used by permission)

When a certain woman came to our church in 1998, she had not been in a church before where bass and drums were played. She did not really prefer the choruses, and she let me know about it. I would visit her apartment in the retirement village (she lives alone) and we would talk about the Word and about Jesus and about prayer. Every now and then she would look at me, eyes sparkling, and say, "Mark, I thank God for bringing me to Antioch. I don't much care for the music, but that's OK. I love the church. I love the people."

She turned 80 a few years ago, and I started telling her that she is my favorite "octogenarian." (Now there is more than one!) Our visits usually include discussions about the church. Many times she cannot come on Sundays because of her health, and she wants to know what's going on and how everyone is doing. Her eyes still sparkle and she still tells me almost every time I come to visit, "Mark, I am so thankful that God brought me to Antioch."

And more than once she has said, "When I first started coming to this church, I loved that the old were together with the young. The children worship the Lord right there with their parents, and the elderly can take part in the service and be loved by the families. But I have to tell you. When I first came to this church, I couldn't stand the banging of those drums. It would bother me sometimes, and it is still not my favorite instrument (smile). But now I love to be there and to sing praises with my family, and it doesn't matter what type of song or what kind of music. I am singing to the One who loves me and who saved my soul!"

Sometimes church conflicts arise from convictions or principles, as it did in our church over whether the best way to 'do church' is to meet in homes. Sometimes church conflicts arise from preferences, as they have in our church over music. Or over whether we will have Sunday School or other weekly 'programs' for the children and youth. We have chosen not to be a program-centered church, and there have been families who left over that issue, and others who would not ever come in the first place!

Whatever the reason, conflict is inevitable. As Job said, ***Man is born to trouble as the sparks fly upward.*** (Job 5:7) A church without conflict is a church without people. Which church, by the way, does not exist!

Sometimes church conflicts arise because of sin. That's when church discipline becomes necessary.

CHAPTER 14

Discipline that Restores

There have been a number of times over the past 18 years when the elders had to exercise church discipline.

One of the elders had a son that was a bit out of control. The other elders asked him to take a sabbatical from the eldership while he restored discipline in the home. He readily agreed, began to spend more time with his son, and we saw a change in that relationship. A healthy elder was able to resume his responsibilities.

Another time found us dealing with a man in the church who wanted to date a woman in the church. Both were separated from their spouses at the time, and we had already spoken with each of them about that, encouraging them to be reconciled in their marriages. When we heard these two were desiring to date, we sat down with him and told him this was not biblical and pleaded with him to turn from this course of action. He refused, as did the woman, and I remember the phone call I made to her (one of the other elders called the man).

"Do you understand what the elders are asking you to do, and that it is biblical and right that you should do it?" I asked.

"I understand what you are asking me to do!" she replied.

"Are you going to do it?" I asked.

"No."

"Are you removing yourself, then, from the fellowship and from the covering of the elders?"

"I am."

My heart was broken for both of them, but our consciences were clear as elders. We explained to the church what had happened and what we had done, and they joined us in grieving for these two and praying for their repentance.

Several years later, the man returned to the church. He was repentant, and we welcomed him back with open arms. Paul said it like this, in Galatians 6:1…

Brethren, if a man is overtaken in any trespass, you who are spiritual restore such a one in a spirit of gentleness, considering yourself lest you also be tempted.

"Restore such a one." That's what Jesus talked about in Matthew 18:15-20, a foundational passage on church discipline.

If he hears you, you have gained your brother.

Amen! When church discipline happens, sin is purged from the fellowship and the guilty person is given over to the Lord to be convicted. But the end result, by God's grace, will be restored fellowship and a brother or sister who has been chastened by the Lord and has repented and matured!

If we do not discipline sin in the church, then we are no different than the world. The testimony of the church will be compromised, and if we continue to wink at sin, I would fear the Lord would come and take our lamp stand away, as He said he would do to the church in Ephesus, unless they would repent (Revelation 2:5).

Several years ago some ladies in our church decided they wanted to lose weight. They had heard great things about a particular weight-loss plan that was very popular with many Christians in America. It seemed to be based on biblical principles for healthy eating and living. One of the ladies sent me a tape to listen to, but I was busy and didn't do it. I skimmed the tape cover, everything looked like it was in order, and so I told them I thought it would be fine. They had done their job, by checking with the elders. We (**I**, to be precise!) had *not* done our job.

They started their group and were meeting weekly to encourage one another, study the Word, and exercise. Then one day after a month or so, I found out that the woman who had written the book and started this national weight loss program was not under biblical authority, had left her church and planned to start a church of her own, and worst of all, she did not believe in the triune Godhead.

There were just two elders at Antioch at the time. I went to the other brother, expressed my concerns and told him that I should have checked it out more thoroughly in the first place. He agreed with me that we needed to act, so we called the woman at Antioch who was hosting the group and asked if we could come to their next meeting. She said, "Sure," and we showed up that next week.

The Bible says that

A soft answer turns away wrath, but a harsh word stirs up anger (Proverbs 15:1).

My first word to these dear ladies was, "I am so sorry." I confessed to them that I had failed to execute my responsibilities and protect the flock as an elder should, and would they please forgive me. We then shared our concerns about the program, and the Lord gave them grace to receive it and they immediately abandoned the program.

Now, I realize that in a best-case scenario, the husbands of these women would have checked out the materials themselves. But sometimes that doesn't happen as it should, and the elders have to step in. I am so thankful for the heart attitude of the ladies (and their husbands, whom we talked to as well), because it could have caused a great deal of anger and resentment. Instead, it caused rejoicing and a turning of hearts toward the Lord and His Word.

There's a key verse from Paul's instructions to Titus that comes to mind. Remember that Paul is writing to Titus, to "set things in order," the FIRST thing of which was to appoint elders. An elder is to be actively

holding fast the faithful word as he has been taught, that he may be able, by sound doctrine, both to exhort and convict those who contradict. (Titus 1:9)

Like a good shepherd, the elders protect the flock of God from those who contradict. Contradict what? *Sound doctrine!* Paul warned the Ephesian elders that they were to

be on guard for yourselves and for all the flock. (Acts 20:17)

The elders are charged to protect the flock, to be alert to danger, to know sound doctrine and be prepared to defend it. How much damage has been done to the church over the ages because of careless, sleepy, and lazy shepherds? How much false teaching has crept into the church over the ages because the shepherds were asleep at the wheel, because they didn't recognize error when it slapped them in the face because they were not familiar enough with the TRUTH. David said in Psalm 119:165,

Great peace have those who love Your law, and nothing causes them to stumble.

First, the elders protect the flock by knowing and loving God's Word. There is nothing more contagious than a Christian who absolutely LOVES God and His Word! When you are around him, it makes you want to KNOW God like he does. And a church that is hungering after God because they are following leadership that is hungering after God has very little chance of going astray. The people fall into error when they see their shepherds asleep at the wheel: that's when the crash happens.

Second, the elders protect the flock by taking action to deal with sin when they see it. A shepherd who is alert to danger and sees a sheep wandering toward a cliff has only done half of his job. The second half is to go and rescue the sheep. Or, try to! Elders who do not practice church discipline are only half obedient to Scripture. Paul said the elders are to...

by sound doctrine, both to exhort and convict those who contradict. (Titus 1:9)

He goes further and says,

For there are many insubordinate, both idle talkers and deceivers, especially those of the circumcision, whose mouths must be stopped, who subvert whole households, teaching things which they ought not, for the sake of dishonest gain...therefore rebuke them sharply, that they may be sound in the faith. (Titus 1:10-11, 13).

Here are some important principles about church discipline.

First, it must be done. The biggest problem with church discipline in the church in America is that it doesn't exist. It's not that it has been tried and found lacking, to paraphrase GK Chesterton, it has been found difficult and left untried.

But if you consider that MOST of Paul's letters were written with that very purpose in mind, to discipline the churches, how can we have strayed so far? Because it is difficult. It requires an eldership that is in the Word, that loves the people, and is unafraid of confrontation. It ALSO requires a people who will support and love and pray for the elders when they administer church discipline. One of the reasons we don't have discipline in the schools anymore is because those who would administer the discipline, the teachers and the principals, have been stripped of that authority by parents and a public who would not support it any more. And the same has happened in the churches.

If the elders do not have the support of the people in exercising leadership that includes church discipline, you might as well go ahead and close the doors.

Second, it must be done in love. Paul said

both to exhort and convict those who contradict in Titus 1:9.

That word for exhort is **parakaleo**, and it means "to urge, beseech, encourage, to call alongside of," for the purpose of giving strength and help. It must be done from a position of love if it's going to work. Jesus loved the rich young ruler even as He was commanding the young man to do the only thing that would disentangle his soul from the things of this world. If Jesus' love is our model, and it is, then we can see from His own life that He didn't shrink from coming alongside anyone to urge, beseech, command, and mostly, LOVE. So, church discipline must be done, and it must be done in love.

Third, it must be done with whatever action necessary.

Whose mouths must be stopped,

Paul said in Titus 1:11! This is not a reference to duct tape, although the word literally means "to put something over their mouths." The source has to be dealt with, firmly and decisively.

Let me ask you parents a question. If your child suddenly came out with something that was completely off the wall at the dinner table, some quote that was worldly or off color or just plain rude, what would be the first thing you would say?

"WHERE did you hear that?!" And suppose you found out that a friend loaned your child a tape of a popular comedian, and your child had been secretly listening to it. What would be the first thing you would do? Take away the tape. You would "stop the mouth" of the offender. And so it is with church discipline. It does the church no good for all of us to patiently overlook false teaching that is spreading through the flock while we petition the Lord in prayer for it to go away. Sometimes we have to take action, especially when, as Paul said, the teaching is being used to *subvert whole households.*

Finally, church discipline must be done to restore the fallen. The last thing Paul says about this matter to Titus is

> *rebuke them sharply, that they may be sound in the faith, not giving heed to Jewish fables and commandments of men who turn from the truth. (Titus 1:13-14).*

But someone may say, "That seems so harsh. Does there have to be a rebuke? Couldn't we all just pray about it and let the Lord deal with it?"

Let me ask you something. Suppose your son was trying to get his little sister to drink a cup of Drano? How would you respond to the little darling? Would you say something like, "Now, Billy, look, Daddy has a sad face on. Will you help Daddy get a happy face again? Will you take that cup away from little sister before she takes a drink? Look, sister's putting it to her lips...Daddy has a sad face...aww come on, Billy...please?!"

Of course you wouldn't respond that way. You would do whatever it takes to save the life of your child! Listen, beloved, it is not "harsh" or "unchristian" to deal firmly with those who reject the truth and who teach others to do so. In fact, not only are you possibly saving whole households from harm, you are also helping that one who is heaping judgment upon himself by leading that household astray. Jesus said it Himself:

> *For offenses must come, but woe to that man through whom the offense comes! (Matthew 18:7)*

Paul said of Hymenaeus and Philetus in 2 Timothy 2:17,

> *their message will spread like cancer.*

If the elders help to cut a cancer away from a man's life, are they being harsh and unloving?

Because we love the church, we MUST take action. Because we love the offender, we must take action, that they may be sound in the faith, and so they will not be in bondage any more. If church discipline is still used somewhere wrongly, the problem lies, perhaps, with shepherds who have lost sight of the goal, a healthy church for the glory of God alone. Instead of healthy church discipline, these 'shepherds' scold the flock to "keep them in line." These leaders may say they love the church, but they really love themselves, and have a hard time with unruly sheep.

This was the rebuke God gave to the shepherds of Israel through the prophet Ezekiel:

*Woe to the shepherds of Israel who feed themselves!
Should not the shepherds feed the flock?...with force
and cruelty you have ruled them...so they were scattered because there was no shepherd.
(Ezekiel 34:2-5).*

Let me close this chapter by paraphrasing again from Doug Phillip's talk, "What to Expect When Establishing a Local Church" ("Uniting Church and Family" Conference, 2003).

He said that there are two things that we need to deal with ahead of time in a new church plant so they do not even get a toe-hold in the foundation.

The first is gossip.

We must remind ourselves and our congregation over and over that

*the tongue is a fire, a world of iniquity. The tongue
defiles the whole body, and sets on fire the course of
nature, and it is set on fire by hell (James 3:6).*

Gossip is the sport of a fool because of its destructive power but can be easily disguised as "spiritual concern." *Have you heard about Tom and Carol's marriage? Hmmm-mmm. They are really struggling. I think, personally, it's because of the affair she had early on....you didn't know about that? Oh, my. Well, I am just telling you so you will know how to pray...*

Although Rachel Lind in the "Anne of Green Gables" story was comic relief, you still want to wring her neck when she is meddling in Anne's affairs or sucking the marrow out of every juicy piece of gossip she can get her hands on.

Gossip can shipwreck a church. The admonition to the congregation must be given continually. I say it at least once a quarter at Antioch: "If you have a problem with someone in the church, the biblical mandate is for you to go to that person directly, *not* to someone else. If someone else has a problem with someone else and he is sharing it with you, then you have a responsibility to stop the talk and send them to the person they have ought against. Otherwise you are participating in that person's sin. Gossip can be defined as 'confessing someone else's sins for him,' but gossip is a sin all by itself. Consider these Scriptures.

> *A talebearer reveals secrets, but he who is of a faithful spirit conceals a matter. (Proverbs 11:13).*
> *The words of a talebearer are as wounds, and they go down into the innermost parts of the belly. (Proverbs 18:8).* In the same way, gossip wounds the body of Christ deeply.
> *Where there is no wood, the fire goes out; and where there is no talebearer, strife ceases. (Proverbs 26:20)*

Now *there's* a verse we need to apply to church struggles!

The second thing that Doug Phillips talked about was the problem of "expectations."

How many of us have come into a church with certain expectations about how the Word would be preached, how the songs would be sung, how the children would behave, how the times of fellowship would be encouraged and facilitated, how the home groups would be conducted...only to have our expectations dashed within the first few weeks? Probably most of us. The question is, what did you do when your expectations were not met?

I called a man yesterday that I haven't seen in church in about a month. Their family had come regularly for about 6 weeks, and then all of a sudden, they were gone. I had emailed and called and had gotten no response, so yesterday I called and said to the voice mail, "I will not bug you anymore. I was just calling to see if you were OK and to tell you that we miss you. Let me know if there's anything I can do for you."

He called me back within a couple of hours and said they had been out of town almost every weekend, but they would be back at church in the next week or so.

"Well, thanks for telling me, brother," I responded. "I wanted to see if maybe we had made you mad or something."

""Not yet," he replied.

This man has a dry sense of humor, and he meant it as a joke. I laughed and said, "That's right, not YET! But, brother, we will, it is inevitable. There will be something we do that disappoints you or makes you mad. It's just a matter of time." He laughed, we chatted some more and then hung up.

If each one of us would come into a church determined to let God be God, then we could let people be people. And people will let you down.

God said it.

> *...let God be true but every man a liar. (Romans 3:4)*

The Psalmist wrote,

> *I said in my haste, "All men are liars." (Psalm 116:11)*

David may have said it in haste, but it's still true!

Church discipline must be done. Sometimes it can be prevented by good teaching and training, which is a form of discipline ("discipling") itself. May God give us wisdom!

We have covered most of the responsibility of the elders when it comes to leading and protecting the flock. There is another responsibility that the elders have, and it cannot be overlooked in a healthy church.

CHAPTER 15

At Home with the Word

T he elders lead the flock, and the elders protect the flock. But there is another very important responsibility of the elders. They are to *feed* the flock. And though there may be lots of diets on the market today that vie for our attention and our dollars, there is only one thing that will *always* nourish our souls and grow us up to

> *the measure of the stature of the fullness of Christ (Ephesians 4:13).*

That is the Word of God.

One of the important cries of the reformers was *sola scriptura!* Literally interpreted "Scripture alone," this phrase means that the Word of God is the only infallible rule for deciding issues of faith and practices. It is a rejection of the belief, held by Catholics among others, that Christian tradition has authority that is equal to or even greater than the Bible.

The Word of God is sufficient. If this is not the very foundation of our church, whether we are 'family-integrated' or not, the church will crumble like the sand that it is built upon.

In fact, it is the very hope that we have in the sufficiency of Scriptures that led us to *become* a family-integrated church. We believe the Word supports family worship and fathers' leadership and biblical eldership, but does not support a "program-driven" philosophy of ministry. We search the Word and cry out to Him who *is* the Word, Jesus, to lead us into all truth.

This book will not attempt to make a case for the veracity of the Scriptures, the reliability of the New Testament manuscripts, or the supernatural way God protected His Word though the centuries. There are numerous books out there that do an excellent job with that.

But I would like to ask this question: if we agree that the Bible is the Word of God, how will that affect how we live?

Paul said it like this in Colossians 3:16-17:

Let the word of Christ dwell in you richly in all wisdom, teaching and admonishing one another in psalms and hymns and spiritual songs, singing with grace in your hearts to the Lord. And whatever you do in word or deed, do all in the name of the Lord Jesus, giving thanks to God the Father through Him.

What does it mean that we are to let the Word of Christ DWELL in us? It is interesting that this word for dwell is different from the word in John 1:14, where we are told,

And the Word was made flesh and DWELT among us.

That word for dwell means "to set up a tent, to 'tabernacle,' to take up temporary residence." But the word for dwell in Colossians 3:15 means "to live in, to take up habitation, to MOVE IN!"

So, even though the second person of the Trinity, Jesus Christ, was only physically on the earth for a few short years, and He "tabernacled" with us for a season until he had accomplished what the Father sent Him to do, His WORD is to take up permanent residence in us. It is supposed to move in. It is supposed to settle down. And it is supposed to be made to "feel at home." Now, let's put a human face on that for a moment.

What happens when somebody feels at home somewhere? Or, what does a person act like in an environment where he does NOT feel at home?

When I visit the Biltmore House in Asheville, NC, it drives me crazy because I like to *experience* something. I can't feel at home there because they won't let me touch the furniture. They won't let me crawl up into Mr. Vanderbilt's bed and see how comfy it is, or swim in his indoor pool, or fix myself a sandwich in his kitchen, or even play a game of billiards. I can look, but I can't touch! Whenever I am there, even though I have had to take out a *loan* to go inside the place, they make it clear that I am *not* welcome to feel at home there.

But then I think about how I felt in my Grandmother's house growing up: we called her Nana. I could walk into the kitchen and get something to eat anytime I wanted. I could use any of the furniture in her house, in fact Cindy and I ended up with a house full of furniture when we first got married that came from Nana's house. When I went over to my grandparents' house, I didn't have to worry about whether I left everything in its place: I could have rearranged her furniture, and it would have been fine with Nana and Granddaddy. I was at home there.

That's what Paul is talking about in Colossians 3. Let the Word of Christ *be at home* in you. Not like it's in the Biltmore, and it's a stranger, not welcome to make suggestions! But let the Word be so comfortable that it could rearrange the furniture and you'd be OK with that. (Even though, sometimes, it is NOT comfortable when the Word starts working on us!)

How comfortable is the Word of Christ in you? I think that's the better question to ask than 'how much Word do you know'? That will *always* lead to a guilt trip. Rather, how much does the Word dwell comfortably in your life? I heard one preacher say that a woman was bragging that she had been through the Bible 37 times. He smiled and said, "But how many times has it been through you?" The question is not, how much Word do you know, but how much Word do you live with? How much has the Word moved in and taken up residence? How much has the Word of God become the measuring rod or the plumb line for everything you believe and do?

Let me warn you! You have got to *watch* that Word of Christ. It won't just take up space, it will *take over*! That's exactly what is supposed to happen, according to this text. That's why it says, "Let the Word of Christ dwell in you *richly*!" (That word means copious, in abundance, plenty of supply).

How would you respond if someone on the street were to ask you, "What do you have in such rich supply at your house that you know you will never run out?"

I remember when we lived in downtown Graham, NC, and we had next door neighbors who loved our kids. They would do anything for our children, and loved them like they were their own. One day one of my sons just walked next door and stood there in the carport until the neighbor lady saw him. She came to the door and opened it. She didn't say anything. She didn't have to. My son said, "What have you got in your house?"

You see, *he* knew that this lady kept an endless supply of cookies in her kitchen and *he* knew she would just *love* to give him one!

What do you have in your house that is in such rich supply that it will never run out? It's not cookies. There's nothing material that we have that will never run out! But the things of God, His love, His peace, His assurance, His Word: these will never run out. We have them in rich supply.

Peter said,

The grass withers and its flower falls away, but the word of the Lord endures forever. (1 Peter 1:24-25).

Have you told the Lord lately that you want to welcome His Word to take up residence in you? Have you offered to Him not the guest room but the whole thing? If that is true about you, then you have probably noticed three very important results in your life. If the Word of God is dwelling in you, and it is really at home as an honored guest, then it will shape how we relate to one another, it will change the way we sing, and it will direct every part of our lives.

It will change the way we relate to one another.

Colossians 3:16 says,

Teaching and admonishing one another.

That doesn't mean every time you pass one of your brothers or sisters in Christ you pull him or her aside and say, "Hey, let me share with you the ten things I learned this week about the Feast of the Trumpets!" No, but what will come out of your mouth will be soaked in the Word of Christ and *that* by itself will teach and encourage and build up and even admonish.

How much at home is the Word of Christ in your conversation? Does it saturate your conversation, or is it just used for seasoning every now and then? Does it try to enter the conversation but you keep it on the sidelines for fear that you might 'offend' or that it might look like you think you are 'something special.' Have you ever read any of the journals or speeches of our founders in America? Their words were seasoned, many times, with the Word of Christ. The words of George

Washington, for example, were usually soaked in Scripture and in biblical principles.

On May 1, 1777 when the news finally arrived that the French would join the War on the side of America, George Washington proclaimed, " It having pleased the Almighty Ruler of the universe to defend the cause of the United American States, and finally to raise up a powerful friend among the princes of the earth, to establish our liberty and independence upon a lasting foundation, it becomes us to set apart a day for gratefully acknowledging the divine goodness, and celebrating the important event, which we owe to His divine interposition."

Once General Washington was visited at his military encampment by some chiefs from a Delaware Indian tribe, and they had brought three youths to be trained in the American schools. Washington assured them with these words: "Congress will look upon them as their own children…you do well to wish to learn our arts and ways of life, and above all, the religion of Jesus Christ. These will make you a greater and happier people than you are. Congress will do everything they can to assist you in this wise intention."

If the Word of Christ dwells in you richly, it will change the way you relate to others. There is a second result.

It will change the way we sing.

It is interesting to me that Paul connects the way the Word dwells in us to the way we sing to one another in *psalms and hymns and spiritual songs*. This is an encouragement to us as churches not to lose the richness of the great hymns of the faith that were, for the most part, written by men and women in whom the Word of Christ dwelt richly! The Psalms, without doubt, were written by men who loved God's Word and were submitted to it. Many of today's choruses (spiritual songs) would fall into that category, as well. There is great power in songs that are rich in the Word of God.

The year was 1780, the place was Springfield, New Jersey. The British were trying to get to Morristown, but the scrappy American Continentals and militia, outnumbered three to one, had been able to hold them back. The fighting was fierce enough, but then it got worse for the Americans as they began to run out of wadding, which was as necessary as the ammunition itself. With the British beginning to press the advantage and push the militia back, Reverend James Caldwell had an idea. He ran into the First Presbyterian Church he served as pastor, and returned with a stack of Watts Hymnals in both arms. Isaac Watts was a familiar name to the soldiers, as the author of such hymns as "O God Our Help in Ages Past," "Joy to the World," and "Am I a Soldier of the Cross."

Distributing the hymnals to the American soldiers and artillerymen so the pages could be used for wadding, Caldwell yelled, "Give 'em Watts, boys!" That became the battle cry that day, and the Americans won. The British retreated, burning and looting the town as they left, leaving only four houses standing. But the American militia had successfully driven them out of New Jersey for good.

If the Word of Christ dwells richly in us, we will sing His praises with psalms and hymns and spiritual songs. Paul says that we will also sing with *grace* in our hearts.

Saints, the more richly the Word dwells in us, the more at home the Word of Christ is in us, the richer and sweeter will be the grace in our hearts with which we sing! I believe the singing of the saint who has grace in his heart, no matter the circumstances, is a powerful thing. When Paul and Silas sang to the Lord in a Philippian jail, their circumstances were rough and unpleasant. But they sang hymns at midnight, they sang with grace to the Lord, and the Lord responded with an earthquake that shook them loose. They weren't singing the blues, dear saints, they were singing praise to God, they were singing a hymn to their Father who had put them in that jail for just that purpose, that His name might be praised, and that the Philippian jailer and his family might come to faith. (Acts 16)

If the Word of Christ dwells richly in us, we will also sing *to the Lord*! There is no comparison between singing to each other and singing to the Lord. Acts 16 tells us that Paul and Silas were singing to God, but the prisoners were listening to them. They were *not* singing to the prisoners, hoping that God was listening. They were singing praise to the Lord, and He heard.

Sing to the Lord. He is worthy of your praise. Sing to the Lord, saints in the congregation. He is worthy. Sing to the Lord, praise team. He is worthy. Sing to the Lord, elders. He alone is worthy!

There is one more thing to consider with this text. When the Word of Christ dwells in us richly,

It will change the way we live.

And whatever you do in word or deed, do all in the name of the Lord Jesus, giving thanks to God the Father through Him. (Colossians 3:17)

The Word of Christ will change everything. As I said earlier, God is not ever interested in just showing up as an indifferent spectator. He comes to take over. When we approach His Word with that understanding, that He is worthy of our complete surrender and our unquestioned obedience, then He will get glory from our every word and every deed.

It is the responsibility of godly elders to model and to teach these truths. The people will have the same reverence and respect for God's Word that they see "walked out" by the leaders. Hebrews 13:7 says,

Remember those who rule over you, who have spoken the Word of God to you, whose faith follow...

May the people of God hear the Word from the elders and be able to clearly follow a trail of obedient faith.

Let me close this chapter with one plea to my friends who are pastor-teachers or elders. In my opinion, the best way to feed the flock is to preach expository sermons. I went for years from one "theme" to another, trying to teach on issues that I thought the body needed. But I found that many times I was coming up with an idea (e.g., "they need to hear about authority!") and then finding verses that seem to support the points I had already decided I would make. Rather than "exposing" what the Bible says and what the author meant and what the situation was and what the context includes, I was simply "imposing" my views and opinions on the text, sometimes even misinterpreting verses to make the point more dramatic. I am so thankful that God did not send a lightning bolt years ago when He could have and probably should have. He was patient with me and taught me a better way.

I believe the best way to preach is to go through large passages of Scripture, if not through whole books. In the past few years I have gone through the major events in *Joshua*, and through the books of *Colossians* and *Philippians*. As I write this book, we are working our way through *1 John*.

I have found that when I am preaching through a book, the mature people are fed the meat and the babes are getting the milk at the same time. I have found that I don't have to 'go looking' for the important themes in the Word, but they will naturally emerge from the Word as I preach the "whole counsel of God." I have found that my preaching is much more God-centered and God-exalting now, and I give Him all the glory. On a practical note, I am thankful that I don't have to spend half the week trying to decide what my *text* will be for the next Sunday. That has already been decided if I am preaching through a book in the Bible.

We have examined the responsibility of the elders in a biblical church. What about the responsibility of the people who follow them?

CHAPTER 16

What's a Body to Do?

O K. I have some good news, and I have some bad news. Which do you want first?

If you are like me, you want the bad news first. If I am eating a piece of cake, I eat most of the cake and just enough icing with it to make it tasty and sweet. Then I eat the best part, the *rest* of the icing! I know some of you out there just have to plow right into the icing first, and you know what your problem is? You just cannot delay your gratification. You have to have it *right now!*

Just kidding. I have heard a lot of people say that they eat the icing with the cake so that every bite is good, and not just the few bites at the end. Others of you have told me (and for the life of me, I will never understand this) that you don't even *like* icing! And you just throw it away! OK, here's the deal. From now on, when you make a cake, call me and I will come and eat the icing for you. Or better, yet, just *send* me the can of icing and don't even put it on the cake to start with! Especially if it's chocolate. Don't get me started...

OK, let me give you the bad news, the *cake*, and then we will get to the icing. Here's the bad news: the congregation has within its power the ability to discourage and deflate and even dislocate the elders. That's it. Leadership is *very* hard work, and those who follow leaders can make it very much *harder*!

They say that good pitching can beat good hitting on most days. But good *leading* can be walloped by bad *following*! That's the bad news, and it's bad.

But there's good news, and it's wonderful. The good news is that the same congregation has within its power the ability to encourage and bless and motivate the elders. Yes! Good leading is great, but good <u>following</u> can create even *better* leading.

Isn't it just like God to make the GOOD news so much "gooder" than the BAD news is bad?

Didn't Paul say,

> *where sin abounded, grace abounded much more? (Romans 5:20)*

Amen! Let's look at a couple of key passages in the New Testament that gives clear instructions to the church on how we are to follow our leaders.

> *And we urge you, brethren, to recognize those who labor among you, and are over you in the Lord and admonish you... (1 Thessalonians 5:12)*

The church is to recognize the leaders.

The word used here for recognize is translated "to know" in the King James Version. It is translated "to appreciate" in the NASV. And it is "to recognize" in the New King James version. Which one is right? Well, they all are. The word in the Greek can be translated as "know, recognize, appreciate," or as "honor or esteem." First, let's agree that it is good for a person in church to KNOW who their leaders are.

It's always funny to me to talk to someone who doesn't go to church but who says that they do. I usually ask him,

"Who are the leaders in your church?" If a person can't come up with the name of one of the elders or the pastor, there's a pretty good indication that person is not involved in the life of that church. I know a lot of the pastors in our county, and sometimes a person who says he goes to such 'n such church will name a pastor who retired 10 years ago, or who went home to be with the Lord 5 years ago. When that happens, I can safely assume that the person I am talking to has not been to church in a lo-o-o-ng time. So, at the very least, this word should mean that we know who our leaders are.

It also means, "to recognize." Would you agree that church members ought to be able to pick their elders out of a police lineup if they had to? (And hopefully they never will!)

We urge you, brethren, to recognize (the leaders). Paul is emphatic: he is urging the church to do something, and I don't think he is urging them to know the names of the elders, or even be able to recognize one of them if they saw him at Wal-Mart.

Perhaps it means, as Strauch suggested in Biblical Eldership (p. 281), that the church should give recognition to and show appreciation for the leaders. He explained that when this text was written in the first century, there was no distinction in the congregation between the leaders and the people who followed them. There were no clerical robes, no collars, no priestly garments, and all for a reason! The leaders of the church in the first century were NOT a separate class, nor should they be now. There is no distinction according to God's grace and economy between the elders and the congregation, and all attempts to make such separations happen in centuries following was a colossal mistake!

At the same time, Paul is saying, let's not forget those who labor among us. So, maybe the word he is using here means to appreciate. It can be translated that way. That goes beyond just knowing the name or the face of the elders, and speaks to a heart attitude of gratefulness. "And we urge you, brethren, to *appreciate* those who labor among you..." Yes, I think we are getting closer to it, now. And then Paul adds this command:

The church is to esteem the leaders.

> *...and to esteem them very highly in love for their work's sake. Be at peace among yourselves. (1 Thessalonians 5:13)*

Paul ratchets it up considerably, here. He uses a word, "esteem," that means "to lead out before the mind." It can also mean leader, or someone who is recognized as having authority. Acts 15:22 says that the apostles and elders chose some men to go with Paul and Barnabus (to deliver the letter to Gentile Christians, telling them they did not have to be circumcised to be a Christian), and they chose *Judas, also called Barsabas, and Silas, <u>leading men</u> among the brethren.* So, to esteem someone is to make a decision with your mind that you will recognize his place of leadership and authority.

But how many of us know that we can do that and still not like it! We can recognize a person of authority with a scowl on our face or a grumble in our heart.

So, Paul adds THREE Greek words here to modify the verb "esteem." It only says two words in English, "very highly," but that's another example of where the English translation just doesn't do it justice. There are three Greek Words here, *huper*, which means "abundantly, more abundantly, beyond measure." Then he adds the word, *ek*, which means, "in full, out of, above, intense." Then Paul adds a third word, *perissos*, and that word means, "exceeding a certain measure, above measure, vehemently!" This is the same word used in John 10:10, when Jesus said

> *But I have come that they may have life, and that they may have it <u>more abundantly.</u>*

What is Paul saying? The church is to esteem the leadership abundantly, intensely, vehemently, with the same measuring cup the Lord used when He said, "I have come to give you life!" A Bible Commentator in the early 1900's, George Findlay, said this verse represents "the strongest intensive possible in the language...so deep and warm should be the affection uniting (leaders) and their flocks." (quoted in Strauch, p. 170, from *The Epistles to the Thessalonians,* The Cambridge Bible for Schools and Colleges: Cambridge University, 1908, p. 117)

William Hendricksen adds, "Note the piling up of prefixes in this word: the ocean of esteem having reached its outermost perimeter, reaches even higher and begins to flow outward, overflowing its banks." (quoted in Strauch, p. 170, from *Exposition of I and II Thessalonians,* New Testament Commentary: Grand Rapids, Baker, 1955, p. 135)

Then Paul does the unthinkable. He adds the finishing touches to it. He says the church is to esteem the leadership very highly *in love!* And not just any kind of love. He uses the word that indicates the highest form of love that we can have for one another, and it is the form of love that most of the world knows nothing about: *Agape.* It is unconditional love. Whenever we love someone unconditionally, we are doing something only GOD can do. Through us, He delights to love His people with no strings attached. That's the way you and I are urged to love the leadership in the church: with no strings attached. Agape love is not based on self; it goes where self cannot follow. It starts where self dies. Agape love sent Jesus to the cross and sends us to our knees in repentance. And that's the love that Paul is urging the church to walk in towards the elders. Unconditional love. To quote Strauch again:

"Believers who love their shepherds will have greater understanding and tolerance for their shepherds' mistakes. In love, believers will view difficult situations in the best possible light. In love, believers will be less critical and more responsive to the elders' instruction and admonition. It cannot be emphasized enough that the best thing a congregation can do for its leaders is to love them. Love suffers long (1 Cor. 13). Love covers a multitude of sins (1 Peter 4:8)." (p. 171-172)

Paul says one final thing about how the church should esteem its leaders. He adds the phrase, *for the work's sake.* This is an important point. Good leadership should provoke this kind of love from those who are being led. But the responsibility of the church is not to esteem elders just because they have a position or a title or even because they like them! The church is to esteem elders because of the work that they do.

Paul ends the verse with this encouragement: *Be at peace among yourselves.* The church is called to recognize those who labor among them, and to esteem them very highly in love for their work's sake. One of the best ways to love the leadership is to walk in peace with one another.

I tell my children sometimes that the best way they can love their Mom and Dad is to love and esteem each other and live in peace with each other. It is the same in the church.

> *Behold, how good and how pleasant it is for brethren to dwell together in unity... (Psalm 133)*

Let's turn now to see what the writer of *Hebrews* has to say about this matter.

> *Remember those who rule over you, who have spoken the word of God to you, whose faith follow, considering the outcome of their conduct. (Hebrews 13: 7)*

The church is to remember the leaders.

What does the writer of Hebrews mean here, when he encourages the believers to *remember* those who lead them? The church is being encouraged to do more than just "remember" that they have leaders, like they would remember that there is a President in the White House.

Look at verse 3 where the writer of Hebrews says,

remember the prisoners as if chained with them.

What are we to do in order to follow this exhortation and "remember" the prisoners as though we ourselves were sitting on the cold floor next to them with leg irons on?

I believe it means that we are to pray for them, to go to them and help if we can, to act on their behalf! And think of this: who are the prisoners he is referring to? They are certainly prisoners who are in chains because of their faith, not because they robbed someone. And they are most likely people who *were* in leadership in some capacity in the church. If that is the case, and we are encouraged to remember them like we were chained in that prison with them, should we do any less for those leaders who are still among us? Should we not also pray for them and go to help them any way we can, and act on their behalf to make their job easier? Should we not rejoice daily for men of God who are taking the heat and running the point for us, who are leading the charge and taking the most intense fire from the enemy? Should we go a week, even a day, without praying for those in authority over us?

One of the things that always surprises me when I am in Africa (or in Haiti) is that when I preach in those places, I seem to have so much more anointing and authority and power. I have had the sensation many times in Africa when I am preaching that I am outside myself, watching myself preach. John Stott, Martyn Lloyd-Jones, Haddon Robinson and other great men of God have commented on this phenomena, this unction of the Holy Spirit that happens sometimes when we are ministering the gospel of Jesus Christ.

But what *is* the source of that extra anointing, that extra power, if you will? Is it something in the preacher? No, I can assure you it is not. But I have a sense of what it might be. When we go on a mission trip, we have a prayer covering from here, with many of the saints praying and praying fervently, *and* we have a prayer covering from <u>there</u>, with many of the African churches praying, and praying fervently! And when we stand up to preach, the enemies' defenses have already been destroyed, and every word finds its target, and walls come crashing down and chains break, and God is there

> *not with persuasive words of human wisdom, but in demonstration of the Spirit and of power. (1 Corinthians 2:4).*

Does He ever do it in the pulpit here? Oh, yes! But I have to confess that sometimes when I am preaching, I feel like I did when I used to try that rope ladder at the fair. You know the one I'm talking about? It has a swivel on both ends, and your challenge is to get on and keep your balance as you walk to the top, which is only about 10 feet away! And every time I have tried it, I knew as soon as I got on that I was going down. And I did. Then the guy running the thing would jump on there and climb up like a monkey, ring the bell, and climb down.

When I am preaching "on the rope ladder," it's a scary thing. Sometimes I am on there because of me. I am not prepared, or prayed up, either as a preacher or as a man of God. And those times lead me to repentance.

But sometimes, I know I have hit a wall of spiritual opposition that should have been dealt with as the church prayed that week. That's one of the reasons why some men of the church are gathering for prayer on Sunday morning at 9. They pray for me, or for whoever is preaching, because this is warfare. And leaders need the heavy artillery to go in before them.

I remember reading once that during the peak of his ministry, there were up to 700 people praying in the basement of the church *while* Charles Spurgeon preached. Every Sunday.

The church is to remember the leaders, and the very best thing you can do for your leaders is to pray. Pray for their intimacy with Christ, because that's always under attack. Pray for their relationship with their wives, because that is always under attack. Pray for their faithfulness in prayer and ministry and study of the Word, because that is always under attack.

But there is more.

The church is to obey and submit to the leaders.

Obey those who rule over you, and be submissive, for they watch out for your souls, as those who must give account. (Hebrews 13:17)

The first word the writer to the Hebrews uses is "obey," and the word literally means "to obey, to listen to, or to follow." I have to hear something in order to obey it. When Solomon asked God for wisdom, he literally asked for an "understanding heart," or a "heart that hears." That's what the writer of *Hebrews* is getting at. The church that hears the leaders' heart and vision with understanding will be MUCH more likely to take the next step and submit.

It's funny, but a marriage works the same way. Peter exhorted husbands to live with their wives *with understanding*, and how many men know that you cannot possibly understand your wife if you are not first willing to *listen* to her? But what was the promise for husbands who do not take the time to listen with understanding to their wives? Neither does God take the time to listen with understanding to their prayers! (1 Peter 3:7).

The first step to a healthy and happy relationship with your friendly neighborhood elders is to listen to them with a desire to understand. That means two things: *give to them* grace because they are imperfect and 'works in progress.' Second, *go to them* when you don't understand or you don't agree. Giving to them and going to them will be a product of that unconditional love that I mentioned earlier in the chapter, and it will build trust.

The second word the writer to the Hebrews uses is "submit," and the word literally means "to yield, to surrender, to cease to fight, to defer to."

John Chrysostom, a church father, wrote, "Anarchy then is an evil, and a cause of ruin, but no less an evil also is disobedience to rulers. For it comes again to the same. For a people not obeying a ruler is like one who has none; and perhaps even worse."

What is the foundational truth about spiritual warfare? "Submit to God." *Then* you can resist the devil and he will flee from you. (James 4:7). There is no organism or system on the earth that works without submission. That is true also in the church; we as

living stones are being built up a spiritual house (1 Peter 2:5).

Again, a quote from Strauch:
"The effectiveness of any body of church leaders is measurably affected by the response of the people they lead. People who are stubborn and unsubmissive are unteachable and incapable of changing for their own good." (p. 269)

I heard of a church once that had a reputation for being a burial ground for good preachers. Every man who tried to lead there ended up being driven away. The church was unreachable, it seemed. And then word got out that things had changed. A man who had left the church years earlier went to visit and was amazed at the transformation. He asked the leadership after the service what happened. There was harmony where there used to be division and strife. There was spiritual power and energy where there used to be carnality and enmity. "How did this happen? What did you do?!" the man asked the pastor. The pastor replied, "First, I preached it down to four." (This helps to prove the adage that it is much easier to give birth than raise the dead. He preached it down to newborn-size and started over!)

Why should the church obey and submit to the leaders? Two reasons are given in the text. First, because the leaders *watch out for your souls.* A healthy church is led by healthy shepherds who labor diligently to protect, feed, lead and care for the flock. They care for the souls of the people in the church. Is there anything more important than your soul? Jesus said,

> *What will it profit a man if he gains the whole world but loses his soul?*

The elders don't look out for your bank account or your job evaluations or even your arteries. They look out for your soul! That word is *psyche*, and it means "you." It's who you really are. You are not your bank account, but a soul. Not that your relationship with your bank account doesn't affect the condition of your soul, it does, and that's why sometimes elders even have to go fishing in your bank account because they care for *you.* But you are not your bank account, you are not your career, you are not your health. You are a spiritual being created in the image of God and will live forever. The elders are called to watch out for your spiritual life, and that's reason enough to obey and submit to them. But there is a second reason.

The elders *must give an account.* My oldest son is in college at "Verity," and he has to stand there on his own two feet. Having said that, his mother and I have been charged with the responsibility for the last 20 years to feed him and lead him and care for him and teach him, and his character is a reflection of God working in his life through his parents and others. We must give an account.

In the same way, elders will be held accountable for the souls God over which gives them stewardship. Paul declared his blameless record of caring for the souls of the Ephesians in Acts 20:26-27:

> *Therefore I testify to you this day, that I am innocent of the blood of all men. For I have not shunned to declare to you the whole counsel of God.*

Because the leaders at Antioch know they we must give an account for souls, we labor more diligently to present them before God as mature and complete. Because they know that we must give an account, we ask that the congregation obey and submit to us joyfully, being willing to lay down preferences for the sake of unity.

If we ask them to come to Sunday morning service with expectant hearts, to be here on time and regularly, we are not asking the saints to do anything except that which we know will be a blessing to them and to us, and bring glory to the Father.

If we ask them to tithe, to give to the household of faith and not rob God, they can do it gladly, knowing that their obedience to God's Word will produce blessing in their lives and in the life of the church, and bring glory to the Father.

If we ask them to place themselves or their family in a home group on Wednesday nights, they can do so knowing that this will help them to grow in the grace and knowledge of our Lord Jesus Christ (2 Peter 3:18), and give glory to the Father.

If we ask them to learn to pray fervently, to seek to know the Word of God and make disciples, to worship the Lord in every word and deed, to put on the Lord Jesus Christ and diligently pursue His character in their own lives, they can do so knowing that this will make them fruitful and cause them to abound in every good work, and bring glory to the Father.

Finally, the writer of Hebrews encourages all of us to follow the leadership that they may give an account for souls

> *with joy and not with grief, for that would be unprofitable for you.*

Every parent knows the extremes our emotions can reach in raising children. Our children have the capacity to bring us tremendous JOY or cause us to sink into the depths of grief. But that's because they're children! Adults should desire to serve under those who lead in a way that brings great joy to them. Let's be truthful, bringing grief to the leadership will certainly not be profitable!

What does it all come down to, in the final analysis? I believe it comes down to "trust." I regularly communicate this idea to the church: "I am asking you all to trust **God** to work through your elders to lead this church."

If the people trust the Lord to work through the elders, they will gladly follow and submit. They are still called to be like the Bereans (Acts 17) and take everything back to the Word of God, which is our standard. I will get a call or an email sometimes from a person in the church who found something in the Word that does not line up with what I said in a sermon. Of course, the Word is right, and I was wrong! I am so thankful that the people of the church feel the freedom to correct me, and do so with gentleness and respect. None of us is above correction and must humbly submit to it as we would to the Lord Himself.

But what if an elder sins? If this happens, the church is given clear instructions to follow in 1 Timothy 5:19-20. An elder who is practicing sin should be publicly rebuked for it. But let's make sure that it is his sin we are dealing with, not his temperament, his personality, his habits or his mannerisms. It must clearly be *sin*. This passage also warns the church not to entertain accusations against an elder without two or three witnesses.

How much more peace and joy would we all have in the church today if the elders led well and the people respected and honored them for it? One of the favorite pastimes in many homes is to enjoy a little "roast preacher" for the Sunday noon meal, but it should not be so! If the elders are faithful shepherds, they should be honored and respected and prayed for and encouraged.

May God give us all grace to do this for His sake.

CHAPTER 17

God or Mammon?

W e were about 3 years old as a church when we made a subtle change in the way we handled our financial responsibilities. Before that time, we ran in the red on a regular basis. Every month was the same. The elders would meet for prayer and to discuss the church and we would go over the financial record.

"We had a pretty good month," the treasurer (a deacon) would say, as he handed out the financial report. "We took in $1450 and spent $1775."

"How was that a good month?" an elder would ask.

"Well, the month before we took in only $1150 and spent $1800," the deacon would reply.

You get the idea. We were going backwards financially, and the only reason we were not belly-up was that one or two of the men in the church were giving substantial amounts whenever they were needed. But there were some problems that we had to address.

There was the age-old problem at Antioch that every church faces. Some were tithing, some were giving but not tithing, some were not giving at all. We have never had to deal with the 20/80 rule, where 20% of the people do 80% of the work.

Most of those who have come to Antioch are laborers who are ready to grow and serve and disciple. Praise God! But the truth is, *most* Americans do not have their financial houses in order and spend more than they make every year. The church is absolutely no different than the world in this regard. So, from the beginning, Antioch has had her share of people struggling with massive debt, and others who wanted to enjoy the benefits of the ministry without investing in it.

I remember it well, the church business meeting we had in the early days to discuss the financial struggles of the church. I was convinced the problem was that many in the body were simply not giving. I did not know then, and I do not know now, who gives and how much they give. I stay out of the loop where that is concerned because I don't want to look at the members of the church as dollar signs. So, I came into the meeting expecting the ones who were not doing their share to confess that, ask for forgiveness, promise to start giving, and ask for prayer that they might be better stewards of their resources. (Oh, how young I was!)

Instead, there was a murmur that what *really* needed to happen was that the pastor (that would be me) needed to be cut back to part-time, and the *pastor* (me, again) needed to get a part-time job to supplement his income. I was crushed. My wife was embarrassed. My kids were oblivious. (They were toddlers, happily playing with their toy trucks on the floor).

I came very close to quitting that day. I felt betrayed by the people I was serving, and angry that not one of them stepped forward and said, "Hey, why are we asking the pastor to get another job. It's *more* than a full time job to serve as our shepherd. Why don't *we* go out and get a part-time job so *we* can make more and give more?"

At the time I did not know that God had a plan, as He always does.

During the next 2 years, I sold World Book encyclopedias door to door. I sold newspaper advertising for a weekly in the county. I helped a brother who put up vinyl siding for a living (he called himself a "plastic surgeon.") Then I got a job teaching at a local university.

In each one of those jobs, God was doing something significant, I believe. The Lord helped me overcome a fear of talking to strangers as I went door to door with encyclopedia and advertising sales. God formed a friendship with the plastic surgeon, and he and his family ended up coming to Antioch where he led worship for nearly 10 years. We learned how to worship because of his influence and leadership. Finally, God opened the door to ministry on the college campus through my job as an instructor, there. He has also allowed me to teach well over 2500 students in 15 years, sharing my life and my passion for truth with them. The Lord has blessed the church with a number of young families who were students at the college and are now members of the church and community.

There is another blessing that came from that business meeting. I have been bi-vocational for 17 of the 18 years I have served as a pastor. The benefits of that position, in my opinion, are more than worth the hassles and the pressures and fatigue. My preaching is more genuine, I believe, because I live in the world of my flock, serving an employer, trying to do my job with excellence, dealing with the problems that are inevitable when you work in the world. Also, when I teach pastor's conferences in parts of Africa, which I have done 4 times so far, I can say to these men: "I know what it means to have to work two jobs and love my wife and train and teach my children." It builds my credibility with these men, 90% of whom are bi-vocational and struggling to keep all the plates spinning at the same time.

So, the business meeting was a turning point for my life and for the church. But there was a second turning point that perhaps is more significant.

In the first two years of Antioch's existence, the bills were always paid as follows: rent, utilities, supplies, miscellaneous expenses, missions' obligations. Finally, if there was money available, the pastor was paid. That meant that many times I would receive my salary check for October...in November! You can imagine how creative my wife and I had to be with our *own* bill paying.

We were in an elders' meeting when one of the leaders said, "You know, I don't think we are looking at this the right way. I mean, it seems to me that we should reverse the order in which we pay our obligations every month. We should pay the pastor and the missionaries *first*, and then if there is money left over, we can pay the rent and other bills. Doesn't God's Word say that the workman is worthy of his hire, and that the ones who sow spiritual things should reap material gain?" (He was referring to Paul's exhortations in 1 Corinthians 9). "Shouldn't we pay *people* first?""

The leadership team agreed with him, and the next month the new plan was put into effect.

Since that time, and it has been 16 years and counting, Antioch Community Church has *never* been in the red again. We have always had a surplus, even though most of those years we have increased our giving to missions and our day to day operational expenses have also increased. God is faithful to keep His Word, and this is just another example of how He showed Himself strong to us.

I believe that a church that is faithful in unrighteous mammon will be entrusted with the true riches—the stewardship of people's lives. We have entrusted at least 15% of our income as a church to the Lord through home and foreign missions, and God has blessed that and increased our giving. The last few years the percentage has been closer to 25% that we have been able to give away and invest in reaching the world with the gospel. To God be the glory! In this area of missions giving as a church, God has shown Himself strong to us as well. All along the way as a church, we have said that the Kingdom of God is not about budgets, buildings, and buses.

It's about people. It's about God's glory being seen by all the world as we are faithful to exalt His name before the nations.

There would be a test of our resolve in 2002, as we were just turning 15 years old as a church.

We had our last Sunday service on the college campus in May of 2002, completing a period of nine years when we were there every Sunday during the school year. The Lord provided a Nazarene church building, built in 1990, for our use. The Nazarenes were building another church facility a few miles away, and they agreed to let us enter into a lease agreement as they moved into temporary quarters while their new place was being completed.

"The only thing is," they told us, "we really want to sell this property. And since your church is not in a position to buy it, we are going to continue to market the property until a buyer comes along. When they do, we will give you 60 days 'right of refusal,' and then sell it to the other buyer if you can't come up with the money."

"OK." We agreed quickly because we believed fundamentally in one clear guiding principle of Scripture. God loves His church. We are a part of His church. God loves us. He will always provide for His own children, and we had every reason to believe that God would provide a meeting place for us. We had met in nine other locations on Sunday mornings since 1987. This "church building" on Powerline Rd. in Elon made number 10, and we believed that if God wanted us to be there, He would make it happen. If not, we would move on.

I remember preaching a sermon from Numbers 9 just a few months before we moved into the new location. It was entitled "When the Cloud Moves," and we saw that great story of God leading His people in the wilderness with a cloud by day and a pillar of fire by night. And God said over and over in that passage that the people were to move "at the command of the

Lord." When the cloud moved, they moved, whether they had been in that location a year, a month, or only one day!

"That is God's call on our life as a people, as a church," I told the congregation that day. "We do not find a place to settle down and then say, 'That's it, Lord. We are not moving again. We are comfortable, here. We move at His command. When the cloud moves, we will move.'"

Sure enough, we had not been in the new location very long before it happened. I got a phone call from the pastor of the Nazarene church (which owned the property we were using), asking if he and his leaders could meet with our elders.

The meeting was short and to the point. The chairman of their board started the conversation:

"Gentleman, as much as I hate to say this, we have an interested buyer for the property. We would much rather see a church remain on this land, but we also have to think about our needs. And our need is to pay off the bank, so we are going to have to accept this offer. Unless..." he said as he paused. "Unless your church would be willing to just go to the bank and get a loan."

The three of us looked at each other and smiled. We had already had this discussion over the past several months, and had decided without any dissension at all that we would look to God rather than man. We believed that God would provide for us as He always had, He would open a door that no man shuts and He would close a door that no man opens.

"Thank you," we responded. "But we will not go to the bank for a loan. We *would* like to have our 60 days to pray and seek the Lord, though."

They agreed and we went to the church the very next day (this meeting was Saturday night) with the report. It looked, with our human eyes, as though the cloud was going to be moving again! To their credit and God's glory, the people took the news without flinching. They had learned what it was like to be a missionary church, picking up and moving as the Lord led, and they were willing to do it again.

About 15 days into our 60 day period, one of the brothers in the church called me and asked what I thought about proclaiming a 40-day fast. I thought it was a wonderful idea, and so did the other elders. We announced it that very Sunday, and asked the people to sign up to fast one or more of the 40 days we had left in the 'right of refusal' period. We asked the church to cry out to the Lord, as the Word says:

> *The righteous cry out, and the Lord hears, and delivers them out of all their troubles." (Psalm 34:17)*

We did just that, and the forty days flew past. I have to admit, I expected God to do something miraculous, like send us a check that would cover the cost of the property. But He didn't do that. The end of the 40 days found us exactly $1000 closer to the purchase price than we were before.

I called the pastor of the Nazarene Church and told him the news, that we would not be able to exercise our option to purchase because we didn't have the money. "But we know God will provide a place for us to meet," I told him.

He assured me that it would still be several months before we would have to move out. The developer would have to do soil testing and then permits would have to be issued and then he could start building.

"I think he could start on the other end of the property," the pastor said. "Then he could bulldoze the building last, so you would be able to stay in there for as many as 6 months, possibly!"

There was one thing in the whole process that the pastor did not mention. He did not bring it up because it was just a formality, a rubber stamp. It was the whole issue of re-zoning. You see, the church building is in a neighborhood, and the whole street was zoned 'single-family.' The developer planned to erect several apartment buildings, so the property would have to be re-zoned as 'multi-family.'

The zoning board refused to do it.

You know, that's just like God. We cried out to Him for 40 days, asking Him to deliver us. We expected Him to deliver us by providing a financial blessing. Instead, he delivered us by turning the hearts of the zoning board. There was no human explanation that I heard from anyone that would satisfy. The town of Elon stood to receive tax revenue, lots of it, if this land was converted from church property (which pays no taxes) to commercial. Still, they refused to re-zone. I don't care what anybody else calls it; I call that a miracle. But there was more.

The Nazarene pastor called and asked if we could meet again. They had decided that since they would not be able to sell the property to a developer, they would let us continue to stay indefinitely and pay rent. Every penny we had paid until that point, and every penny we would pay in the future would go towards the purchase price of the property! Not only that, but they agreed to give us an exit clause so that if, two years from now, or ten years from now, the cloud moves, we could get out of the lease with no penalty. We would pay no interest at all, we would never have to borrow money, and the monthly lease price would be reasonable and lower than the going rate for commercial property.

When the church heard the news the next time we gathered for worship, they rejoiced in what the Lord had done. To this day, whenever I tell that story, the hearer is amazed at what the Lord did. "That's a miracle!" is the response I most often hear.

And it is.

CHAPTER 18

The Great Commission

I heard about a man who was going off to join the Army, but he was in love with a young girl and didn't want to lose her. "I am going to write a letter to you every day," he promised. "You wait for me!"

And he was good to his word. He wrote her 365 letters that year, one a day. And then he was horrified to find out that his girl was getting married...to the *mailman*!

There is NO substitute for the personal delivery of the message. Jesus didn't send a message, He came in person. He didn't tell the disciples to *send* a message, He sent the disciples.

One day the great evangelist D.L. Moody asked a stranger on the street, "Are you a Christian?" The man looked at him and curled his lip and said, "Mind your own business!" Moody answered, "This *is* my business." The man said, "Then you must be Moody."

That story convicts me to the soles of my feet. Am I known as a person in Burlington whose *business* it is to witness? If I am minding my own business, then I *will* be telling people the good news. As Jesus said to His parents,

Did you not know that I must be about My Father's business? (Luke 2:49)

You and I, also, are called to be about the Father's business, and reaching out to lost and dying people is a large part of that!

One of the questions that I get from people who are looking askance at the "family-integrated church" movement is this: "How does a church like that do outreach?"

I think it is a legitimate question. There is a tendency for any church to become inwardly focused very quickly. It even happened to the church that we hold up as a model, the first church in Jerusalem.

Remember, the Lord's last command to the church before He ascended was to

Go therefore and make disciples of all the nations, baptizing them in the name of the Father, and of the Son, and of the Holy Spirit, teaching them to observe all things that I have commanded you; and lo, I am with you always, even to the end of the age. (Matthew 28:19-20)

That was spoken before the Day of Pentecost. About 40 days later, the church was born as the Holy Spirit came and they all received power to be witnesses to Christ

in Jerusalem, and in all Judea and Samaria, and to the end of the earth. (Acts 1:8).

The church exploded with growth, and thousands were converted on the first day after Peter had preached to the Jews who were in Jerusalem on the Day of Pentecost. Then thousands more were added as you follow the growth of the early church through the first 7 chapters of the book of Acts. Several years went by, and the church prospered...in Jerusalem.

The church was not sending out missionaries to all of Judea, much less Samaria. And forget about the "uttermost parts of the earth!" It was all very exciting in Jerusalem, and though there were some conflicts they had to deal with (more about church conflicts later), the first church was making no moves at all toward obeying *all* of the Great Commission.

God was not going to sit idly by and watch that happen.

Whenever the church has been stagnant in its witness over the years, God does something about it. To use the language of the "Perspectives on the World Christian Movement" we sponsored at Antioch in 2004, God uses "voluntary go," "involuntary go," "voluntary come," and "involuntary come."

For example, He called Abram to leave Ur of the Chaldeans and go to a place that he had never seen. Abram voluntarily left his home and moved, and the rest is history, as God blessed Abraham and made him a nation.

God took Joseph into slavery and to Egypt, where he would become a savior of the Hebrews. Joseph did not go voluntarily, but as he said later to his brothers...

you meant evil against me, but God meant it for good, in order to bring it about as it is this day, to save many people alive. (Genesis 50:20).

The Vikings invaded Christian Europe in A.D. 800-1200, and "were conquered themselves by the faith of their captives." (Perspectives on the World Christian Movement, Study Guide, by Steven C. Hawthorne. Page 51). The European Christians were terrified of the savage Vikings, and would not go consistently to them with a witness. So, God brought the Vikings to the Christians.

Then there were countless slaves who were forced to come to America or other places where Christianity is practiced. Though they came against their will, and because of the sin of slavery, many ended up finding life through Jesus Christ as a result.

The point of the teaching in the "Perspectives" course is this: God, who has commanded us to take the gospel into all the world, will make sure that it is done. Jesus said,

I have a baptism to be baptized with, and how distressed I am till it is accomplished! (Luke 12:50).

Jesus wasn't talking there about His baptism with water, but His baptism with fire, as He went to the cross and purchased our lives with His blood. Why did He do that? Because God loves the world. God is

not willing that any should perish but that all should come to repentance. (2 Peter 3:9).

It is with that understanding that we read in Acts 8:1,

At that time a great persecution arose against the church which was at Jerusalem; and they were scattered throughout the regions of Judea and Samaria, except the apostles.

God saw that the church was comfortable, enjoying the blessings of fellowship and growth, which it should have done. But He also saw that they were complacent, not taking the gospel to every creature in all of Judea and Samaria and the uttermost parts of the earth! So, He turned up the heat. Persecution is not a tool of the devil but a gift from God. As the saying goes, the blood of the martyrs is the seed of the church. Wherever the church is persecuted, it grows and matures. Wherever the church is comfortable, it grows inward and complacent.

Now, we cannot manufacture persecution, nor should we! That is part of God's job description, not ours. But as believers who trust God and love His Word, we must do all that we have been commanded to do so that God will not *have* to bring persecution.

How does a "family-integrated church" obey the Great Commission, then? I think the answer to that question will be as varied as the churches that respond to it. Many churches have programs of evangelism, training the people how to use the Evangelism Explosion method, for example. That's fine. Others stress friendship evangelism and encourage their flock to make friends with sinners. As they build a relationship at work or at school, they are establishing a platform from which they can speak into that sinner's life at some future point. That's fine. Others encourage revival meetings and crusade evangelism. They get involved in hosting or helping to host an evangelist who will come to their city and preach the gospel to thousands, and the workers in the local churches follow up and disciple those who "make a decision." That's fine. Others believe that witnessing takes place best when they invite people into their homes. They use hospitality as the mechanism, inviting sinners to a meal and then sharing the gospel with them if it seems good. That's fine. Others believe strongly in "lifestyle evangelism." They say that their method of witnessing is to let their light so shine before men so that they may see their good works and glorify the Father in heaven. That's fine. Perhaps the most effective and most often forgotten method of evangelism takes place with our own children, as we lead them to the understanding that they are born in sin and must surrender to Jesus Christ for salvation.

I remember Ray Comfort talking about how he preaches to sinners in the open air and shares the truth of the Word with them, that

He has appointed a day on which He will judge the world in righteousness by the Man whom He has ordained. (Acts 17:31).

A well-meaning Christian approached him afterward and said, "I don't like the way you do evangelism."

"Why not?" Ray asked.

"You are standing out here on the street, preaching to perfect strangers, for one thing," the man replied. "And besides that, your message is too heavy and depressing. You talk about the law of God. You tell them they are sinners and you talk about hell and judgment and damnation."

"That's because it is truth, and it is the way Jesus preached to sinners who were not broken already by the law, "Ray answered. "You don't offer a man grace until he first understands that he needs it. You don't try to save a drowning man unless he knows that he is drowning. Otherwise he will rebuff your efforts or even hate you. But let him see that he is dying, *then* grab his hand, and he will allow you to take him to safety with a grateful heart."

"I still don't like the way you do evangelism," the man persisted.

"How do *you* do it?" Ray asked.

"I don't do it at all," the man answered.

"I like my way *much* better than yours," Ray replied.

Do you see? The argument is not what method we choose. I believe that some methods are better than others, but all of the methods I have mentioned have been used with great success over the years. The question is, will we *do* it?

I have read lots of books about witnessing. I have listened to scores of tapes and CDs. I have even gone through a video course, training me how to present the gospel.

It still comes down to obedience.

I heard someone say once, "If you never catch a fish, can you call yourself a fisherman?"

Wow. That hurt. Got me right in the heart. Brought tears to my eyes.

If I never lead someone to Christ, can I call myself a witness? Can I say I am obeying Christ's command to go and make disciples if I never make a disciple?

An orange tree is supposed to produce oranges. An apple tree is supposed to produce apples. A grape vine is supposed to produce grapes. When these trees or vines do not produce what they are supposed to produce, we say there is something wrong with them. We may prune them. We may spray them. We may even pull them out of the ground and throw them on the compost heap.

What does a Christian produce? The answer, according to Christ's Great Commission, is "other Christians." I know, I know. Some of you are reading that and thinking, "Only GOD can make a Christian!" That's true. Only God can make a tree, too. But God uses people like me and you to dig the earth, plant the acorn, water it, and He gives it life and brings it out of the earth.

I believe this whole area of obeying the Great Commission is one of the greatest problems in the modern church. It has become, to our shame, the Great *Omission*.

Part of it is a theological problem. The church that does not believe that it is the responsibility of the believer to take the gospel

to every creature (Mark 16:15)

will not strive to do it. The church that does not believe we

must all appear before the judgment seat of Christ, that each one may receive the things done in the body, according to what he has done, whether good or bad, (2 Corinthians 5:10)

will not urge its members to witness. The church that believes it is the responsibility of the "hired guns," the "trained professionals" to witness, and therefore the ordinary believer is relieved of his responsibility…will not encourage and teach the people to do it. God gives leaders to the church

> *for the equipping of the saints for the work of ministry, (Ephesians 4:12),*

NOT to do the ministry while the church looks on and approves or does not approve. Church is *NOT* a spectator sport!

So, though much of the problem can be laid at the feet of wrong "orthodoxy," or beliefs, that is not the key. I believe the key is not orthodoxy but orthopraxy, or, "wrong practice."

We know what to do, we just don't do it.

We are like the little boy who wanted to be Jesus in the church drama. He got his wish, the director of the drama asked him to play the part of Jesus. And then the time came for him to act out the part where Jesus had to go to the cross. The little boy ran from the room.

When the director found him, he asked what the boy what was wrong.

"I don't want to play Jesus any more," the boy said through his sobs.

"But I thought you wanted to play this part," the director said. "Why don't you want to be Jesus anymore?"

"I don't want to die!" the little boy said.

It's the same with me. I want to play the part as long as it is fun and comfortable and easy and exciting. But I don't want to die! And in order for me to witness, especially to a stranger, I have to die to my own desires and live for His. I have decided that, at least for me, the first step is the hardest.

There is a Chinese proverb that says, "A thousand mile journey must begin with the first step."

I remember when I sold <u>World Book</u> encyclopedias door to door to supplement my income as a pastor. The hardest thing to do every morning was get in the car and drive to a neighborhood and knock on strangers' doors. Everything in me militated against taking that first step out of the car. Sometimes I would sit in the car in front of a house for 5 or 10 minutes, until I was convinced that if I didn't go ahead and get out, the neighbors were going to be calling the police about this "guy sitting in the car like he's casing the neighborhood."

I would finally summon my courage, reminding myself of a wife, 2 children, and one on the way who were depending on me to put milk and bread on the table. Taking that first step out of the car and onto the sidewalk was all I needed. After that, it was easy. I didn't mind talking to the person who opened the door. I believed in my product and could sell it. Once I took that first step, I was OK.

The same thing happens to me when I get ready to write a column for the *Daily Times-News* of Burlington, NC each week. I can easily spend 30 minutes just staring at my computer, trying to figure out what I should write about. Sometimes that staring is made more productive through prayer, but I admit that sometimes it is closer to catatonia than conversation. But when I finally get started, once I take the first step, I am on my way and the words sometimes even seem to write themselves.

Taking the first step to inviting someone over from the church for dinner might be the key to building fellowship. Deciding you are going to really clean out the garage is not enough. You have to take the first step...into the garage! Making up your mind that you will witness to someone tomorrow is a great idea. But great ideas lay dormant unless and until the first step is taken. Having a desire to play the piano is epidemic. The numbers dwindle, however, when you count those who take the first step, or, lesson. Wanting to see your family settled into a good church is a wonderful 'want.'

It will only happen when you turn that want into action and take the first step.

Sometimes taking the first step even results in God's miraculous intervention. Take the children of Israel and their entrance into the Promised Land, for example. God commanded the priests who carried the Ark of the Covenant to take the first step into the Jordan River. This was during flood stage so the water would have been deep and swift. The promise that would attend to their obedience was clearly spelled out by God's word:

> *...as soon as the soles of (your) feet...shall rest in the waters of the Jordan, the waters of the Jordan shall be cut off...and they shall stand as a heap. (Joshua 3:13).*

That first step was the hardest because it required faith. But God enables us to act in faith and then God rewards faith with his power! The waters stood that day on either side like a wall of testimony to God's faithfulness.

What God has promised will come to pass, but sometimes he lays down conditions for his blessings. In this case, it was that his followers take the first step. It is not only the hardest step, but the most important one as well.

Here are some things you can do in your church to encourage your people to take that first step. And I have to confess that this is an area, like many others, that we still struggle with at Antioch. We are learning what it means to be a Great Commission church. We have *not* arrived.

- Offer a "Perspectives" course at your church. Go to www.perspectives.org to find a class near you or to schedule one for your church. It will give your church an expanded vision for how God has taken the gospel to every corner of the globe, and the job that remains!

- Take people on short-term mission trips. I believe that we need to be good stewards of God's resources, so this can be overdone. But I have seen young people come back from a short-term mission trip with a "world vision" that they did not have before they went. I have seen people get bolder in their witness to a neighbor in America because they have witnessed to a crowd in Haiti or Africa. They also come back with a desire to give to missions and to help others "go."

- Encourage those in your church who are actively obeying the Great Commission to share with the church how they do it. Enlist their help in training others in the church who are willing to learn. The 2 Timothy 2:2 principle of discipleship does not just apply to teaching doctrine but also applies to training behavior and lifestyle. *And the things that you have heard from me among many witnesses, commit these to faithful men who will be able to teach others also.*

- Invest in some good resources and encourage your home groups to go through them. I recommend anything written by Ray Comfort, and his video series, "The Way of the Master," is excellent. Go to www.livingwaters.com for more information about his ministry and resources.

- Model it yourself, if you are a pastor or a church leader. I believe a key verse for discipleship is what Jesus said of Himself and His Father: *Then Jesus answered and said to them, "Most assuredly, I say to you, the Son can do nothing of Himself, but what He sees the Father do; for whatever He does, the Son also does in like manner.*

(John 5:19) The people of the church will follow the leadership of the church. That's the way it is supposed to be. If I am not modeling a lifestyle of evangelism for the people of the congregation, then I cannot blame them if they are simply following my lead! I try to go out once a week by myself or with another brother and witness on the street, in the park, or in the neighborhoods.

- Read great books from men and women of God who had a passion for Him that would not be quenched. These are men and women who have made the greatest impact on the world, even though their lives may have been short. I am thinking of saints such as Oswald Chambers, Hudson Taylor, David Brainerd, Martin Luther, John Calvin, John Wesley, Charles Spurgeon, Charles Finney, Amy Carmichael, Jim and Elisabeth Elliot. There are many more that you can add to the list. I also recommend the books of John Piper, a contemporary pastor whose books provoke a passion for Christ and a desire to find our joy in God. His book, <u>Don't Waste Your Life</u> will challenge you!

- Pray. Get a passion for souls on your knees.

CHAPTER 19

Multiplication, Not Addition!

One of the reasons we named our church *Antioch* is because we like the model presented by the original *Antioch Church* in Acts 13. They were multi-cultural, Spirit-led, and missions-minded. The first time this church is mentioned in the Scriptures, they are sending out a missionary team to travel the known world and plant churches. Not only that, the team consisted of two of their five leaders, Paul and Barnabus.

The church at Antioch believed a simple principle of mathematics and a powerful principle of the Word of God: multiplication trumps addition, *any time!*

Let me put it to you this way. If you had the choice between receiving one million dollars or receiving a penny today and doubling that amount for 30 days, which would you choose? It is hard to even imagine that in 30 days, you would receive enough pennies to make it worth your while. It would probably be *much better* to take the cool million, right?

Wrong! If you were given a penny today, 2 pennies tomorrow, 4 pennies the third day, and kept getting double the amount 30 days…your final "income" would be more than a *billion* pennies. The total amount would be $10,737,418.23. That's almost eleven million dollars!

What does that have to do with the church?

Everything.

Were we called to go out and "add to the church" and see how many fish we could fit into the aquarium? Were we called by God to keep tearing down our barns to build bigger ones? Does the church with the most people meeting in the same place on Sunday morning "win?"

If that were God's plan, I am convinced He would have told Paul and Barnabus to stay right where they were and see if they could get 'ol Antioch to become the finest 'mega-church' on the planet!

I believe God would have us follow the model of the early church, once they were scattered by persecution. Everywhere they went, they took the gospel and planted churches.

Our church sponsors a man in Zimbabwe by the name of Simon Mkolo. He grew up in that country and has lived his whole life there. In the 1960's, before Simon was saved, he was thrown into prison for stirring up dissent against racial prejudice and injustice. To stop his mouth from preaching insurrection against the government, the officers imprisoned Mkolo for 4 years.

It was the best thing that ever happened to him. Perhaps it was the best thing that happened to Zimbabwe in the 20th century.

During the last year of his imprisonment, Simon met an African pastor who shared with him that Christ is the only one who can set men free and establish justice and peace on the earth. He gave Simon a book to read, and shortly after that, Mkolo repented of his sins and trusted Christ to be his savior.

Simon came out of prison with a new purpose. Instead of traveling the country to agitate against British colonialism, Simon Mkolo began to walk from village to village, sharing a much more powerful message. He preached the Kingdom of God and forgiveness of sin and life eternal through Jesus

Christ. "Unless a man is born again," Simon preached, "he cannot see the Kingdom of God." (John 3:3).

There were many who heard the message and responded with faith. Simon would stay in the village until he had trained them in the foundations of the Christian faith, and helped them to establish a new church. There were others who were not so welcoming, however.

"You will not preach in my village," one man said, teeth clenched in anger. "I will chop your neck with an axe if you do!"

Simon ignored the threat, and preached the Gospel to the entire village. The man with the axe and the murderous intent was one of the first to convert.

Simon continued to preach, traveling by foot from village to village. He had been a coal miner before, and the family lived on low wages. Now life became more difficult but Simon believed he was to depend on the Lord for his income. There were many times that his wife, Maina, went to the cupboard only to find it bare. Once when she had no food in the house, Maina began to boil water, believing the Lord would provide. As the water came to a boil, there was a knock on her door, and a neighbor had come over with food. "I believe the Lord would have me share this with you," she said. (source: www. newdirections.org)

When I met Simon and Maina Mkolo in 1999, our church had already been sponsoring their ministry for 11 years, giving through New Directions International in Graham, NC. I was in Zimbabwe with JL Williams and several others, and had the privilege to participate in the dedication of one of the churches Simon Mkolo had planted. He is one of the most humble, unassuming, unpretentious men I have ever met. Completely unimpressed with himself and his accomplishments, Simon greeted me as though I were visiting royalty.

But Simon is the one who has planted more than 300 churches. More than three hundred. There are tens of thousands in the struggling nation of Zimbabwe who owe their spiritual heritage to God's grace poured out through Simon Mkolo.

I tell you that story because I stand amazed at how God has used one man's witness to reach a nation. Like a latter-day Paul, Simon Mkolo has simply obeyed the Great Commission and taken the gospel to where the need is.

My desire is that Antioch Community Church would do the same thing. We have sent out some families to be a part of other churches. Some have *gone out* to be a part of other churches (smile). But our desire is to plant family-integrated churches in our surrounding counties, or even in other parts of the world.

Our vision is to continue to grow until there are around 250 people who are faithfully committed to the church here. Then we would desire to send out two elders and their families, along with 4-6 other families, to start a new work. We want the church to be a *sister*, not a daughter. That distinction will allow the new church plant to find its own identity with our support, encouragement, and counsel (as needed).

Right now the church has around 215 people who are committed to it, and so we should be able to move towards a church plant in the next year or so, Lord willing. But the Lord may continue to bring new people in as He moves a family here or there through job transfers or through different visions. Whatever He decides!

CHAPTER 20

What Does it LOOK Like?

I will close the book with a peek at a typical Sunday morning
at Antioch. That has been one of the questions I have been
asked most often by family, friends, and by people at home
school conferences where I have spoken on the 'family-integrated church.'

"What does it look like?"

It was the same question we used to get about home
schooling. "What does it look like? How do you do it?"

Or about having seven children. "What does a typical day
look like when you have a large family?" (Actually, when my
students at the university find out I have seven children, they ask
these three questions, usually in this order: "Are you Catholic?"
No. "Are you a Mormon?" No. "Are you *crazy*?" Maybe! But I
prefer to think that we are blessed.)

Here's a typical service, beginning at 7:30 when the elders
meet.

The elders gather in my office every Sunday morning (except
the third Sunday) at 7:30am. On the third Sunday of every month,
we meet with the shepherds (home group leaders), 16 men, at

6:45am, followed by a Men's Breakfast for all the men and young men of the church, 12 years and up.

On the Sundays that the elders meet, we will begin with prayer, believing that God would have us come to Him in worship and adoration, and also to humbly submit to His will for the church. After a season of prayer, we will begin to discuss the matters of importance for that day or that month. I will usually have an 'agenda' planned out, but each one of the elders can present an item for discussion at any time. Sometimes we will search the Scriptures together for answers, sometimes we will plan future ministry, and sometimes we will make decisions regarding missions or other financial matters. On occasion, someone will come to meet with us at 8:30 or so for counsel or because we need *his* advice on a matter. The elders meet together for 90 minutes, from 7:30 until 9:00am. That is a crucial time for us to make sure we are in agreement and moving together toward the same goals. It is also a time for us to share burdens, to hold each other accountable for struggles we are facing, and to pray personally for each other. I know that the other elders love me and will speak truth into my life when they see a problem or have a concern, and I will do the same for each of them. It is a rich blessing to serve alongside these godly men!

The worship team arrives at 9:00am and practices the music for that morning for 45 minutes. The worship leader (we have several, but one who is 'primary') will come in with a song list, and we are blessed to have gifted musicians who can learn quickly and play skillfully.

There are also several other activities that may be happening at the nine o'clock hour. One of the elders has been meeting every Sunday for several years with young men ages 12-18 who want to study the Bible with him. The fathers are invited and encouraged to be in there and to participate. I may be teaching a New Members' Class at that hour, or teaching a Bible Study for anyone who wants to come. In the fall of 2005, for example, I taught a class on Hermeneutics and Homiletics for those in our church who wanted to learn more about how to 'rightly divide the Word.' There is also a Men's Prayer meeting at 9am. For a season, there was a class for young ladies, aged 12-18 that a few of the Moms led. They took them through a particular book, and the other Moms in the church were invited to participate. All of this, and more, can be happening between 9 and 9:45.

The worship service begins at 10:00, and we have greeters at the front door with bulletins beginning at 9:45. There is a family who is doing this ministry of greeting, and they are recruiting others to join them. We want those who arrive to see joyful smiles on friendly people who welcome them to the gathering of God's people at Antioch!

The service will usually begin with me greeting the people from the platform, encouraging them to enter into a place of worship in their hearts. I may read a Scripture passage (just a verse or two, usually) and comment on it as I welcome the people and invite them into the Lord's presence. We will pray, and then the music team will lead in song.

During the singing, all of the families and singles are worshiping the Lord together. There is no nursery during this time, and babies' squealing blends right in with our voices raised to Him in praise.

After 25-30 minutes of worship singing, the songs will come to a close. One of the men of the church will stand at the front as everyone is in an attitude of worship, and he will ask us to come to the Lord at that moment for a time of cleansing. We believe that God uses the time of praise and worship to plow up the soil of the heart, and in that tender moment when we are looking at His gloriousness, His holiness and beauty, it is normal for us to see how stained we are, how much in need of confession we are. During those few minutes, we are led to a place of asking the Lord to search us and try our hearts, and we take that time to confess our sins to Him, confident He will cleanse us (1 John 1:9).

When the brother closes in prayer after our time of quiet confession, the people will sit and prepare to hear the Word. At this time, Moms or Dads can slip out quietly with an infant and take him or her to the nursery if they choose to do so. (Most parents choose to keep their children with them in the service). The nursery workers for that day will be there and ready.

I will come to the platform (from where I was worshiping the Lord with my family, in the congregation) if I am preaching that day. I will welcome the people again, invite the visitors to fill out a card and put it in the offering plate later, and then I will begin to preach. The people will stand with me as I read the text for the day, followed by a prayer.

I like to use Power Point with my sermons, because I know that in the congregation every Sunday there are auditory learners *and* visual learners. (There are kinesthetic learners, too, but we can only hope that they will take the bulletin insert we provide every week that is a blank piece of cardstock, and take notes!) The Power Point is normally a simple outline, but on occasion I will include a picture or graphic, if it is helpful. For example, when I preached on 1 Samuel 17, I showed the folks a picture of the Valley of Elah, where David and Goliath actually fought. Well, where *David* fought. Goliath just talked loud and then died!

I will preach for 40-50 minutes, usually, and most of the time I will open it up for questions or testimony immediately after. This has been such a blessing because it gives the people of God an opportunity to hear from Him as He speaks through *anyone* in the congregation that day who has a word that will emphasize or even complete what I have been preaching!

If the Lord leads, I will issue an invitation after I preach for people to respond by coming forward for prayer, but this does not happen every Sunday.

After the sermon, we will take communion together, if it is the first Sunday of the month. We are considering taking the Lord's Supper more often, but have not moved in that direction as of yet.

After communion (or after the sermon), one of the other men of the church will lead the congregation in a time of "thanksgivings." We have done this since day one at Antioch, and it has always been a time of blessing and encouragement. The brother who is leading has a handheld microphone and will take it to anyone in the congregation who has something to share. The people know this time is coming every Sunday, and so they are usually prepared. We have heard everything from birthday announcements to witnessing stories to a new job to a new baby on the way to a testimony of God's miraculous intervention or healing to something a child said that week that blessed the family. You name it. But it has almost always been something that edifies the body and glorifies the Lord. Very rarely has anyone taken advantage of this opportunity to share something in the flesh or to promote an idea that is not biblical. When that *has* happened, the elders have corrected it gently, and the church obviously has survived! No, the church has <u>thrived</u> because of this open time of ministry. Everyone at Antioch knows that church is not a spectator sport, but a gathering of the priesthood. They come prepared to minister. (Some do NOT come to Antioch precisely because it is a church where you are expected to participate at some level. Bu this is not a church where you can come in and hide on the back row and not get involved.)

At some point during the sharing time, the leader will ask the ushers to come and receive the offering. The ushers can range from fathers to teens to younger boys of 9 or 10 years old. During the offering, we may have a special song, or even an occasional liturgical dance that is offered as a sacrifice of praise to the Lord.

When the sharing time is over, there will be an opportunity for anyone to give an announcement or a prayer request. This may also be the time that we introduce a new family or single that has gone through the New Members Class and desires to join. Or a family has a new baby they want to have dedicated by the elders. Or we may pray for a brother who is going to Iraq. Or for a family going on a short-term missions trip. Or for someone who is sick and is calling for the elders to anoint with oil and pray, as James 5 teaches. Whatever we are praying for, the elders are there to lead, but anyone in the congregation who wants to join us up front to pray is welcome and invited to do so.

I will close the service with a time of prayer, and then I will speak the blessing of Numbers 6:24-26 over the congregation:

The LORD bless you and keep you;
The LORD make His face shine upon you,
and be gracious to you;
The LORD lift up His countenance upon you,
and give you peace.

With that, the final AMEN is said and the people are dismissed.

Vance Havner used to say, "Most churches start at 11:00 sharp and end at 12:00 dull."

We start at 10:00. But we never end at 12:00 dull. We end at 11:45 or 12:00 or sometimes even 12:15, but the body of Christ has been sharpened and encouraged in their faith. They usually linger for 20-30 minutes to talk and hug and enjoy the love of the fellowship we have in Christ.

After the service we may have a meal together. We encourage people to bring a covered dish and stay after church for fellowship around the tables. Usually 5-10 families, sometimes more, will stay. At least once a month, we encourage everyone to stay for lunch. We may have a special event happening, like a baby shower that everyone is invited to in the fellowship hall as we eat lunch. Or we may have a slide show in the sanctuary after lunch where we get an "end of the year review" of all God did that year through pictures and music. Sometimes we may have a big volleyball game after lunch. But on these Sundays when everyone is encouraged to stay, we usually have 150-180 people who will sit down together and eat. That's a special time to get to know the families or singles that are new or 'new to you!'

I leave the house on Sunday mornings at 6:45am or earlier. I don't get home most Sundays until after 2pm. It makes for a long day, but I love it.

They say the true test of a good church is whether the pastor would go there if it wasn't his job. I don't know if that's the "true test" or not, but I will say this:

I cannot imagine being anyplace else this side of heaven. Should the Lord choose to send me and my family somewhere else some day, I will go. But until that time comes, if it ever does, Antioch Community Church is where you will find me.

I love this place!

J. Mark Fox
July 22, 2005

Afterword

W hen I finished the first draft of this book, I breathed a sigh of relief, and whispered a heartfelt "Thank You" to the Lord. He is the One who has given the vision, He is the One who has energized His people, He is the One who has accomplished this work that we call Antioch Community Church. To God be the glory. He has done a great work and deserves all of the praise.

I also want to observe that there are as many different ways to "do" family-integrated church" as there *are* family-integrated churches! If I have led you to believe in any way that what God is doing here at Antioch is the final word or the finished product or the best way, I humbly ask you to forgive me. We are a work in progress. We have a long way to go. We are being refined by God and He is changing us even as I type this sentence. There are *many* family-integrated churches out there, and we are just one among the multitude.

I also believe that what God is doing at Antioch Community Church and at many other local fellowships is much bigger than the label, "family-integrated" can encompass. It is a work of family and church reformation. He is calling us to a *biblical* model, I believe, and that is why there is blessing and fruit wherever there is obedience. I imagine that there will be hundreds, perhaps thousands, of new churches planted over the next few years that will call themselves *family-integrated.* They will be different in many, many ways. But my prayer is that there will be a desire and a dogged determination in each one to hold up the Scripture as sufficient and as a model for how to fellowship and disciple and witness and pray and teach and shepherd. That will be glorious, Christ-honoring, and exciting!

Finally, I could not begin to express how much gratitude I feel in my heart for my wife. If God has been able to use me in spite of my weaknesses and sin to help shepherd Antioch Community Church, He has *greatly* used Cindy to encourage me, pray for me, love me, counsel me, and stand by my side. At the same time that she has been a helpmeet to me in every sense of that biblical word, she has been an example to the other women of the church. God has used her servant's heart to bless and encourage others to follow her example. Paul encouraged Timothy to let his "progress" be evident to all. My wife is a faithful follower of Jesus Christ whose progress and spiritual maturity and humility and winsomeness has been and *is* an example to many. For that, and for her, I give God glory.

I hope this book has been helpful to you. I would love to hear from you if you have questions. I would also love to hear of your own progress with working to build a biblical church that honors God and equips families. Please email me at markfox@antiochchurch.cc or visit our website at www. antiochchurch.cc

May the Lord richly bless you as you follow Him with all your heart.

J. Mark Fox

Printed in the United States
107546LV00001B/280-285/A